CHE GUEVARA

THE CUBAN STYLE OF REVOLUTION

ABHILASH CHAUBEY

Contents

CHAPTER ONE

Introduction

E rnesto Guevara de la Serna, commonly known as "Che Guevara," "El Che," or just "Che," is arguably one of the most famous revolutionaries in world history, certainly in the history of the last century or more. In January 2000, *Time* magazine named him one of the 100 most infl uential people of the 20th century, and the famous photograph that Alberto Korda took of Che, entitled "Guerrillero Heroico" (Heroic Guerrilla Fighter) has been called "the most famous photograph in the world and a symbol of the 20th century" (BBC News 2001). His name, his ideals, and his romantic image have become part of the spirit and symbolism of those who believe that the social injustices and worst forms of human exploitation in this world can be erased only by revolutionary means. Rarely in history has a single fi gure been so passionately and universally accepted as the personifi cation of revolutionary idealism and practice. Moreover, even those who feel no sympathy for the ideals he upheld continue to be affected by the charisma of his historical persona and the enduring legacy of his revolutionary life.

He personifi ed the revolutionary ferment that swept the world during the momentous decades of tumultuous change that shook the world during the 1960s and 1970s.

Thus, a prominent Mexican political writer

(who was the foreign minister of Mexico from 2000 to 2003) has written the following about Che: "Many of us today owe the few attractive and redeeming features of our existence to the sixties, and Che Guevara personifi es that era . . . better than anyone" (Castañeda 1997:410). More important, however, is since his death in 1967, Che's defi ant and charismatic image in the 1960s' photographs of him has become an almost universal symbol of revolution and resistance to social injustice around the globe (Anderson 1998:xiv). Che's iconic face appears on posters, banners, billboards, fl ags, books, periodicals, murals, Web sites, T-shirts, and walls in every region of the world. Indeed, his face and to a lesser extent his name are known to people of all ages everywhere.

Che Guevara continues to be regarded by millions of people as a heroic fi gure because of his legendary revolutionary life and his selfsacrifi ce for his revolutionary beliefs. He was a man who not only lived by his principles but died fi ghting for them. Four decades after his death, he remains a fi gure of veneration among the oppressed, young rebels, radical intellectuals, social activists, revolutionaries, guerrilla fi ghters of all kinds, and the international global justice movement (often referred to by the mainstream media as the anti-globalization movement). He is also hated and vilifi ed by many people in high places and in Cuban-exile communities throughout the Americas which remain vehemently opposed to the socialist government of Cuba and to the role played by Che in this government: fi rst as one of the most outstanding leaders of the revolutionary guerrilla war that brought this government to power and subsequently as one of the most internationally famous leaders of Cuba's new socialist government and champion of expanding Cuban-style socialist revolutions throughout the rest of Latin America and the world.

T oday, he is widely perceived in Latin America as "the herald" of a region-wide social revolution (Taibo 1997:10), which many Latin Americans believe is as urgently needed today as it was in the 1960s when Che gave his life fi ghting for this cause. In fact, the idealistic origins of this cause can be traced back to the 1800s, when many of the inhabitants of the region rose up in rebellions and revolutions against foreign domination, colonialism, slavery, and ethnic discrimination (particularly the extreme forms of discrimination suffered by the AfroLatino and indigenous peoples of the Americas).

There is increasing interest throughout Latin America in his revolutionary example and ideals due to the continuing social injustices, extreme social inequality, chronic poverty, and political corruption in the region as well as the rise of new leftist political movements and the election of popular leftist governments throughout Latin America. In response to this growing resurgence of interest in Che's revolutionary life and the 40th anniversary of his death (October 9, 2007), a two-part biographical feature fi lm directed by the well-known Hollywood director, screenwriter, and cinematographer Steven Soderbergh was released in 2008 at the Cannes Film Festival in France. Moreover, to memorialize in 2007 the 40th anniversary of his death and in 2008 the 80th anniversary of his birth, many international conferences and public events were held around the world, especially in Latin America and Europe.

T he extensive body of recent literature (hundreds of books and thousands of articles), video documentaries, Hollywood fi lms, Web sites, songs, poems, and works of popular art on Che Guevara have ensured that his legend lives on and that he is known to people all over the world. Many of his own writings have been published, translated into many languages, and read by people of all ages. In fact, Che's revolutionary legend has grown as the years have passed since his death in 1967, and many of the revolutionary ideals that he lived and died for now appeal to a new generation of 21st-century men and women around the world, particularly in Latin America.

T he continued political importance of his revolutionary example and ideals can be found nearly everywhere in contemporary Latin America, especially in socialist Cuba but also in Central and South America. His revolutionary image and many of his ideals have been adopted by the Zapatista liberation movement in Mexico; the newly elected leftist leaders and governments in Bolivia, Ecuador, Nicaragua, and Venezuela; and the international global justice movement, which is composed of hundreds of environmental, women's, indigenous peoples, fair trade, radical labor, and peace and social justice organizations around the world. Indeed, the familiar revolutionary political slogan "¡Che vive!" (Che lives!), which was shouted in the 1960s and early 1970s at antiwar protests and political demonstrations and painted as political graffi ti on walls and buildings around the world, has as much political signifi cance today in Latin America and the Caribbean as it did in the past.

This book provides a comprehensive account of all aspects and periods of Che Guevara's life. It is for readers who know very little about him as well as those who know something about him and want to know more. It provides a chronological account of his life, starting with his early life in Argentina during the 1930s, 1940s, and early 1950s; his travels throughout Latin America during the early 1950s; the important role he played in the Cuban Revolution during the late 1950s and early 1960s; his unsuccessful revolutionary mission to Africa in 1965; his last revolutionary mission, in Bolivia, during 1966–1967; and the circumstances surrounding his death on October 9, 1967. It also discusses Che's contributions to the theory and tactics of revolutionary warfare and socialist theory and practice.

Among other things, this book reveals that in addition to being a famous revolutionary and international political fi gure, over the course of his life Che was a road and materials analyst, medical research assistant, ship's nurse, traveling salesman, street photographer, doctor, author, head of the Central Bank of Cuba, military commander, director of Cuba's Central Planning Board, minister of industry, and an important foreign statesman. This book also reveals a great deal about his family life, his likes and dislikes, personality traits, and the most important people in his life. Moreover, it provides a great deal of information about the geography, history, politics, economics, and social problems of Latin America that were the context for his life and his contemporary legacy.

T his book does not focus exclusively on the life and the death of Che Guevara. It also includes an account of the fascinating story behind the publication of his Bolivian campaign diary, which was taken from him when he was captured and killed by elements of the Bolivian army. Moreover, this account of the posthumous publication of his diary is followed by the equally fascinating story of how his body, which was secretly buried after he was killed, was discovered in Bolivia and transferred to Cuba in 1997—30 years after his death.

The last chapters of this book examine how Che has been celebrated and held up as a revolutionary hero by the government leaders and people of socialist Cuba and by the new leftist political leaders, movements, and governments that have emerged in Latin America in recent years. Thus, the last two chapters of the book focus on Che's enduring political legacy and the important contemporary political infl uence of his revolutionary example and ideals throughout Latin America and the Caribbean.

Readers of this book are encouraged to approach the subjects discussed in the following pages with compassionate objectivity. Adopting this perspective is especially advisable for those readers who have had the good fortune to be raised in relatively affl uent and secure living conditions and who now are fortunate enough to fi nd themselves living in comparatively stable and nonthreatening political, economic, and social circumstances. Unlike these readers, the majority of humanity has been raised in poverty, and they are now living in relatively unstable, impoverished, and threatening political, economic, and social circumstances. Consequently, their views of the world around them and their aspirations and frustrations are quite different from the views and aspirations of the minority of humanity who live in affl uence and relative security. For this reason, they are more willing to support revolutionary leaders and movements that promise to improve their living conditions and circumstances through the violent overthrow of the existing social order.

Che's life provides an excellent case study of how individuals become revolutionaries—how the conditions and circumstances in which they live can lead them to follow this path. Che Guevara the revolutionary was molded by specifi c historical circumstances, societal conditions, and sociopsychological factors. The term "revolutionary" conjures up in the minds of many people a stereotype of a wild-eyed, bearded extremist who is driven by some fanatical urge to destroy the existing order of things, no matter what the cost in human life and property. Che Guevara does not fi t this stereotype. In order to understand why Che became a revolutionary and why he died as one, it is necessary to put aside any preconceptions one has about revolutionaries and examine carefully his life and circumstances. Only by examining carefully the life of this remarkable man is it possible to gain insight into why he became a famous revolutionary and why he died a tragic death as a revolutionary guerrilla fi ghter in Bolivia at the age of 39.

To understand why men and women like Che Guevara choose to live and die as revolutionaries, it is also necessary to recognize that the mainstream media's coverage of subjects such as revolutions, revolutionaries, socialism, communism, democracy, poverty, guerrilla fi ghters, terrorism, Latin America, imperialism, the role of the U.S. government in international affairs, and many of the other subjects discussed in this book often provides a quite biased and misleading perspective on these subjects (see NACLA). One of the main reasons their coverage is biased and misleading is because they tend to frame, or explain, these subjects using a culturally and politically ethnocentric perspective.

T hat is to say, they present the world from a middle-class (and above) North American or European cultural and political perspective, and they rarely present alternative views of the world from other social-class, cultural, or political perspectives. Moreover, they often do not provide adequate or accurate information on the political, economic, social, and cultural circumstances in which the majority of the people in Latin America (and Africa, the Middle East, and Asia) live. Apart from inaccurate reporting, they often misrepresent historical processes and report on political leaders, social movements, and political events using a narrative that refl ects the fear of change and perceptions held by those who hold power and enjoy many privileges rather than the views and interests of those who have little power and few or no privileges (see NACLA). Consequently, they do not do a good job of presenting the often radically different and opposing views people in this important region hold on subjects such as the ruling political and economic elites, social inequality and social justice, revolution and revolutionaries, socialism and capitalism, democracy and oligarchy, the military and police, poverty and human insecurity, and the role of the U.S. government and large transnational corporations in the affairs of their countries and the region.

I n order to understand the conditions, circumstances, people, and events that shaped Che's life, it is important to have at least a basic understanding of Latin America's history, politics, economies, cultures, and social problems. In this regard, it is important to understand fi rst of all that there is no single, uniform pattern of characteristics that fi ts all the countries of Latin America (Harris 2008). In fact, there are considerable differences between the 20 countries usually considered to make up this region. There are differences in terms of the size of these countries. The biggest by population and territory are Brazil, Mexico, and Argentina, which are some of the largest countries in the world, while the smallest are countries such as Panama,

Costa Rica, and Uruguay, which are some of the smallest in the world. They are all multicultural societies, but they differ in terms of the ethnic and cultural composition of their populations—some Latin American countries such as Bolivia, Mexico, and Ecuador have large indigenous (Indian) populations while others, such as Haiti, Cuba, and Brazil, have a large number of people of African descent. They also differ greatly in terms of their geography. For example, Bolivia and Paraguay are landlocked countries in the center of the South American continent, while Cuba, Haiti, and the Dominican Republic are located on tropical islands in the Caribbean; and some countries like Brazil and Mexico have lots of natural resources, while others such as Uruguay and Haiti have very few natural resources.

They differ greatly in terms of their extent of industrialization (e.g., Argentina, Brazil, and Mexico are the most industrialized, while Bolivia, Haiti, and Nicaragua are some of the least industrialized in the Americas, and in terms of their main exports (for example, Venezuela's main exports are oil and bauxite, while Chile's main exports are copper and fruit, and Guatemala's main exports are coffee, sugar, and bananas). Moreover, they differ in terms of their relations with the United States and each other. Thus, the governments of Cuba and Venezuela, which consider Che to be a revolutionary hero, have relatively close relations with each other but relatively hostile relations with the government of the United States, while the government of Mexico has more or less friendly relations with the government of the United States but strained relations with the governments of Venezuela and Cuba.

T he Latin American countries also differ considerably in terms of how unequal the distribution of their total national income is among the population (Harris 2008:52).

The income of the richest 20 percent of the population is 40 times the income of the poorest 20 percent of the population in Bolivia, whereas in Uruguay and Venezuela the income of the richest 20 percent is approximately 11 times the income of the poorest 20 percent. For Latin America as a whole, the income of the richest 20 percent of the population is 19 times the income of the poorest 20 percent. By world standards, this 19-to-1 ratio of unequal distribution is quite high and is one of the reasons why Latin America is considered the region with the greatest social inequality and why Che Guevara believed a socialist revolution was needed in Latin America. In contrast, in the United States the income of the richest 20 percent of the population is about 8 times the income of the poorest 20 percent, which is considered relatively high for an advanced industrial country; for example, the ratio in Canada is only 5.5 to 1.

D espite their differences, however, the Latin American countries do share many characteristics and conditions. In fact, the differences that exist between the Latin American countries do not detract from the importance of their commonalities. With the exception of socialist Cuba (where most sectors of the economy were placed under state control in the early 1960s), all the Latin American countries have capitalist economies, and these economies all hold a subordinate status in the global economic order (Harris 2008). This subordinate status has to do with their historical development—they have all been shaped by the same international economic and political forces over the last 500 years. That is to say, they all have a history of European colonial conquest and domination, slavery, and other extreme forms of labor exploitation. Their economies were established under European colonial rule, primarily to produce and send agricultural products or mineral resources to the European markets of their colonial masters. In addition, their political systems were created to serve the interests of their colonial rulers and then, after colonial rule came to an end, to serve the interests of their wealthy landowning elites (called "oligarchies") rather than the general population. As a result they have inherited government institutions such as the military and police that have strong authoritarian and repressive tendencies. This is one of the main reasons Che Guevara thought that an armed revolution was needed to bring about progressive change in Latin America.

The economies of the region have all undergone a similar process of highly uneven, inequitable, and foreign-dominated economic development over the last 500 years (Harris 2008). And over the last 100 years, this form of distorted economic development, which has been variously labeled with terms such as "underdevelopment" or "dependent development," has produced an unstable and slower rate of economic growth and more frequent and more severe economic crises than has been the case in the advanced industrial countries of the United States of America, western Europe, and Japan. In this regard, many critical thinkers in Latin America and elsewhere, Che Guevara included, have argued that these countries were able to develop faster and create more advanced industrial economies because they have done so at the expense of the Latin American (and African, Middle Eastern, and Asian) countries, which have supplied them with cheap natural resources, cheap agricultural goods, and cheap labor as a result of the unfair prices and unfair trade relations imposed on them by the now advanced countries (Chilcote 2003).

S ince the end of World War II (and even before this in many countries of the region), the most important sectors of the Latin American economies have been dominated by transnational corporations and foreign investors with home bases in North America, western Europe, or Japan. In addition, most of the Latin American countries are burdened by large foreign debt owed to large international private banks and the three powerful intergovernmental fi nancial institutions that operate in the region—the International Monetary Fund, the World Bank, and the Inter-American Development Bank. These three intergovernmental fi nancial institutions are heavily infl uenced by the U.S. government and together they tend to promote the interests of the large transnational corporations and foreign investors that are involved in the economies of the Latin American region. And, again, all the Latin American countries have been historically handicapped by unfavorable terms of trade that give unfair advantages to the more advanced industrial countries that dominate the global economic system. This situation was criticized by Che Guevara in his writings, speeches, and relations with government offi cials and leaders of countries around the world.

After World War II, the increasingly powerful transnational corporations based in the United States and in some of the other advanced industrial countries invested heavily in Latin American economies to take advantage of their abundant supply of natural resources, cheap labor, lax environmental regulations, and captive consumer markets (Harris 2008). Over the last several decades, these powerful corporations and the international fi nancial institutions mentioned above have promoted what they call the increasing integration of the Latin American economies into the global economic system, which is dominated by these very same corporations and fi nancial institutions. Consequently, the most profi table sectors of the Latin American economies generally are dominated by these transnational corporations and foreign investors. These economies are also excessively dependent on the limited number of products they export to the advanced industrial countries, rather than producing products for their domestic markets, and as a result most of the Latin American countries trade more with the United States and other advanced industrial economies than with each other.

Along with these common economic traits these countries have other, more distressing similarities. In most of these countries, a large percentage of the population lives in poverty, there is widespread unemployment, and a large sector of the population is forced into the so-called informal economy in which they are precariously employed as street peddlers, small vendors, domestic workers, and day laborers or engaged in illegal commercial activity such as prostitution or drug traffi cking (Harris and Nef 2008). The majority of the workers in the so-called formal sector of these economies are low-skilled and semiskilled workers, who receive much lower wages and many fewer benefi ts (if any) than comparable workers in the advanced industrial economies.

Moreover, because a large percentage of the population is either unemployed, underemployed in temporary and part-time jobs, precariously employed in the informal sector, or engaged in subsistence or semi-subsistence agriculture, these economies are also characterized by the kind of unequal distribution of income mentioned above. That is to say, the majority of the population receives a small fraction of the total income of these societies, while the wealthy elites receive a major proportion of the total income and own most of the land. This unequal distribution of income and land is coupled with the increasing concentration of other forms of wealth (personal property, stock ownership, etc.) in the hands of the relatively small elite, who form the top layer of the steep pyramidal class structures that exist throughout Latin America. Indeed, there is a growing polarization and income gap between the extremely wealthy upper classes at the top of these class structures and the middle and lower classes below them. As a result of this unequal distribution of income and wealth, there is extensive poverty, social exclusion, and political inequality throughout Latin America.

These distressing characteristics of Latin American countries have been criticized for a long time as immoral and unjust by progressive thinkers, social activists, and critical intellectuals—particularly from the middle and working classes. Che Guevara was a progressive thinker who became personally outraged by the social inequality, political oppression, social injustice, class discrimination, political corruption, and forms of foreign domination he saw in his travels around Latin America. Trained as medical doctor in his native Argentina to heal the sick and do no harm, Che's social consciousness and humanitarianism were challenged by his experiences on the road, where he encountered widespread poverty, social inequality, exploitation, discrimination, political repression, and the diseases and ill health caused by these unjust conditions.

H e was greatly infl uenced by these experiences as well as the political events, leaders, and situations he witnessed fi rsthand in Latin America and the practical political education he received as a result of his participation in many of these events and situations. In the following pages,

Che's observations and insights, convictions, opinions, and actions will be examined in relation to the circumstances, events, ideas, prominent intellectuals, and political leaders he encountered over the course of his adult life in Latin America and around the world.

CHAPTER TWO

Guevara's Early Life in Argentina

Che Guevara was born on May 14, 1928 (although his birth certifi cate indicates he was born a month later, on June 14, 1928), in the Argentine city of Rosario, which is located in northern Argentina on the famous Paraná River. His parents named him Ernesto (his father's fi rst name) and as is the custom throughout most of Latin America, his full name consisted of both his father's family name and his mother's family name. Thus, as a boy and young man he was known as Ernesto Guevara de la Serna—Guevara being his father's family name and de la Serna being his mother's family name. Since he did not assume the fi rst name of Che until much later in his life, in this chapter and the following two chapters, he will be referred to as Ernesto Guevara.

His parents were of upper-class origin. His father, Ernesto Guevara Lynch, was an entrepreneur and a builder-architect who studied architecture but never received his degree. During the more entrepreneurial phase of his career, he tried his hand at ranching, yacht building, and the cultivation of maté (the herbal tea that is the national drink in Argentina). However, he ended up as a builder-architect. His ancestry was both Spanish (Guevara) and

Irish (Lynch) and one of his great-grandfathers was one of the wealthiest men in South America

(Anderson 1997:4), but over the years the Guevara family lost most of their wealth. Ernesto's (Che's) great-grandfather Juan Antonio Guevara left Argentina for the gold rush in California, where he married a beautiful Mexican woman named Concepción Castro. Their son, Roberto Guevara Castro, was born in California but returned with his parents to Argentina, where he married Ana Isabel Lynch, who was also born in California. She was the daughter of an Argentine family of Irish ancestry that like the Guevaras went to California during the gold rush but returned later to Argentina. Their son, Ernesto Guevara Lynch, was Ernesto's (Che's) father. During Ernesto's (Che's) childhood, he loved listening to his grandmother Ana Isabel's tales of frontier life in California.

His mother, Celia de la Serna y Llosa, came from a wealthy landowning family of Spanish ancestry. Her parents died when she was quite young, and as a result she received a sizable inheritance at the age of 21, which was the same year Ernesto was born. She graduated from an exclusive Catholic girls' school in Buenos Aires. She was an intelligent, quite literate, unconventional, and generous person who remained devoted to Ernesto, her fi rstborn, until her death just a few years before his own.

S oon after Ernesto's birth, his parents moved to San Isidro, Argentina, where Ernesto's father was a partner in a yacht-building business. It was while they were living in this city along the banks of the La Plata River that his parents discovered the young Ernesto had asthma (which he suffered from the rest of his life). His mother was an avid swimmer and used to take him with her to the yacht club in San Isidro when she went swimming. On one particularly chilly day, by the time she was ready to leave the club she discovered he was very ill. She and her husband took him immediately to a local doctor, who informed them that their son had a severe asthmatic condition. For the next two years, Che's parents tried every possible cure, but in the end they were advised that they would have to move to a much drier climate if they wanted their son's health to improve. As a result, they moved to the little town of Alta Gracia on the gentle western slopes of the Sierra Chica in the central Argentine province of Córdoba.

E rnesto grew up in Alta Gracia and later in the provincial capital city of Córdoba, along with his two brothers and two sisters, who were born there. The dry climate of the region greatly benefi ted his health, although he continued to suffer periodic asthma attacks, which at times forced him to stay in bed for days. Nevertheless, as he grew older, Ernesto spent as much time outdoors as possible. His childhood friends recall that he was always organizing hikes to the hills and playing games requiring physical skill and endurance (Caligiuri and Piccon 2007). He learned to swim at an early age, and this sport became one of his passions. His parents, especially his mother, encouraged him to swim, since they believed this sport would improve his health and particularly his breathing problems. As he grew older, he also became an avid golfer and loved to ride horses.

H is friends remember him as a decisive and bold youth who was very sure of himself (Caligiuri and Piccon 2007). He had several nicknames during his childhood. His family members often called him "Tete," while his friends called him "Ernestito," "Fuser," and "Chancho." His childhood and school friends remember him for his enthusiasm, mischievous and courageous nature, and adventurousness. Evidently, he was a real daredevil, willing to do almost anything, perhaps to prove to himself that in spite of his chronic illness he was just as good or better at doing things as his friends. Enrique Martin, one of his childhood friends, remembers him as a "real friend when somebody needed him" and as "a charismatic person" who "never got angry more than two minutes." According to Martin: "We all respected and admired him for his kindness" (Caligiuri and Piccon 2007:52).

T he family rented various houses in Alta Gracia, but the house where they spent the most time was Villa Nydia, which is today the Museo Casa del Che Guevara (Museum of Che Guevara's House). The family lived in Villa Nydia from 1935 to 1937 and again from 1939 to 1943 (Caligiuri and Piccon 2007:41). It is the house that was most thought of by the Guevara family as their home in Alta Gracia.

E rnesto's family life was relatively happy, although his parents separated when he was a young adult. His father gave him considerable freedom and moral support. His mother gave him a great deal of love and attention; they had a special bond between them. Ernesto always confi ded in her, even years later when he became an important leader in the Cuban Revolution. Because of his asthma, he was unable to attend school during the fi rst years of his primary education (Caligiuri and Piccon 2007:72). During this period, his mother tutored him at home, and Ernesto spent hours reading alone or playing chess with his father. Later on, when he was enrolled in school, his mother taught him to speak and read French, in which he was fl uent. By this time the frequency of his asthmatic attacks had decreased considerably, and his attendance in secondary school was quite regular.

A. espite his asthma, as he grew older Ernesto became involved in a wide variety of outdoor activities and sports. He swam, played soccer and golf, rode horses, took up target shooting, and loved biking and hiking (Anderson 1997:18). Although he sometimes had to be carried home by his friends because of an asthma attack, he was determined to do everything his friends could do and refused to let his asthma limit him. The administrator of his primary school, Elba Rossi de Oviedo, remembered him as a "mischievous boy" who exhibited leadership qualities on the playground (Anderson 1997:19). She said: "Many children followed him during recess. He was a leader, but not an arrogant person. Sometimes he climbed up trees in the schoolyard." She also said he was "an intelligent and independent person," who "had the qualities necessary to lead a group," and "he never sat at the same desk in the classroom, he needed all of them" (Caligiuri and Piccon 2007:72).

Ernesto's parents wanted their children to be freethinkers. At home, the parents never spoke of religion except to occasionally criticize the conservative hierarchy of the Catholic Church, and the children were given considerable freedom to think and talk about all kinds of subjects as well as indiscriminately associate with people from all classes (Caligiuri and Piccon 2007). They were given no religious instruction, and his parents asked that their children be excused from religion classes in school. Although he was baptized as a Roman Catholic when he was an infant to please his grandparents, Ernesto was never confi rmed as a member of the church. His parents, especially his father, were critical of the hypocritical role played by the conservative Catholic clergy in Latin American society. They felt strongly that their children should not be overprotected and that they should learn about life's secrets and dangers at an early age.

Their home life was somewhat Bohemian, and they followed few social conventions (Anderson 1997:20). Ernesto's mother, Celia, challenged the prevailing gender norms for women in Alta Gracia and was a liberated woman for her time. She was the fi rst woman in town to drive a car, wear trousers, and smoke cigarettes in public. She was able to get away with breaking many of the social norms in the socially conservative community because of her social standing and generosity. She regularly transported her children and their friends to school in the family car and started a daily free-milk program in the school for the poorer children, which she paid for herself.

E. rnesto's father considered Celia to be "imprudent from birth" and "attracted to danger" and chided her for passing these character traits on to her son (Anderson:21). rnesto's father in turn was known to have an Irish temper, and it appears he passed this trait on to Ernesto, who as a child could become "uncontrollable with rage" if he felt he was treated unjustly. In temperament, however, Ernesto was more like his mother, who was his confi dant and at times his co-conspirator in criticizing what they considered to be the hypocritical and outmoded social norms of their provincial community.

E rnesto enjoyed playing soccer (or football as it is called in Latin America and most of the world) and rugby. In the former sport, he usually played the position of goalkeeper, always with an inhaler for his asthma in his pocket. However, it was at rugby that he really excelled. Hugo Gambini, in his biography of Che, claims that the position he played as a youth in this game helped to define his personality (Gambini 1968:18). It seems he played the position of forward, which is generally the key position in rugby since the majority of advances depend on it. Ernesto played this position fearlessly, as though both his personality and his physical attributes had been made to order for it. Perhaps, as Gambini suggests, this game was instrumental in shaping Ernesto's personality as a daring leader.

All those who knew Ernesto Guevara as a youth were impressed by his intelligence and the ease with which he learned new things. However, he was not an exceptional student and he was not interested in getting high grades in school, since his interests lay outside of school. He was preoccupied with hiking, football, rugby, and chess. In the case of chess, he was an excellent player and it became his main hobby. Ernesto also was an avid reader. From his father he developed a love for books on adventure and history, especially the works of Jules Verne (Taibo 1996:24), and from his mother he gained a love for fi ction literature, philosophy, and poetry. He had read nearly every book in his parents' relatively large home library by the time he was in his early adolescence.

E rnesto grew up in a highly politicized environment. Both his mother and father identifi ed with the leftist Republican cause during the Spanish Civil War, and after the war they became close friends with two Spanish Republican families who had been forced to fl ee Spain and seek exile in Argentina after the fall of the republic when the dictatorship of General Francisco Franco was established. The Guevara family was also fi ercely anti-Nazi. His father belonged to an anti-Nazi and proAllies organization called Acción Argentina, and Ernesto joined the youth wing of this organization when he was 11 (Anderson 1997:23). His mother formed a committee to send clothes and food to Charles de Gaulle's Free French forces during World War II. She was leftist in her political orientation and far more progressive minded in her political views than his father, who was more of a libertarian conservative. However, both of Che's parents strongly opposed the spread of fascism in Europe (and Argentina) and opposed the popular military strongman Juan Perón as he rose to political power in Argentina. During the presidency of Perón, Ernesto's mother was an outspoken critic of this famous Argentine political leader and the mass political movement called Peronism that he created in Argentina.

B ecause of his parents' active support for the Republican cause in Spain and the Allied countries fi ghting against fascism in Europe during World War II, and their opposition to Peronism in Argentina after the war, Ernesto was caught up in his parents' political activities at a crucial time in the early formation of his political consciousness (Anderson:23–25). His family's involvement in anti-fascist and antiPeronist politics helped shape his view of the world as well as his political ideals and views.

A ccording to those who knew him as a youth, many of the character traits for which he became famous as an adult were already present when he was a boy: "physical fearlessness, inclination to lead others, stubbornness, competitive spirit, and self-discipline" (Anderson 1997:21). However, at this stage in his life, his interest in politics was secondary to his other interests.

In the summer of 1943, Ernesto and his family moved from Alta Gracia to the nearby city of Córdoba, to which he was already commuting daily by bus to attend a secondary school more liberal than the one in Alta Gracia. Largely because of his mother's wishes, their home in Córdoba had the same casual open-door policy as their home in Alta Gracia. All the friends and acquaintances of the Guevara children were always welcome, there was no regular schedule for meals and they ate when they were hungry, and there was nearly always a wide assortment of interesting guests (Anderson:27). Although the Guevaras welcomed everyone into their home, Ernesto and his mother would tease mercilessly any visitor who showed any pretentiousness, snobbery, or pompous behavior.

A mong the new friends Ernesto made in Córdoba were two brothers, Tomás and Alberto Granado (Taibo:25). Tomás was Ernesto's schoolmate, and Alberto was Tomás's older brother. Alberto was a fi rstyear student in biochemistry and pharmacology at the University of Córdoba when they fi rst met. He was also the coach of a local rugby team. Even though Ernesto was relatively inexperienced and his father was afraid he would suffer a heart attack from playing such a strenuous sport, Ernesto convinced Alberto to let him join the team; he soon earned a reputation for being a fearless rugby player despite his frequent asthma attacks. Alberto was impressed by his fearlessness and his determination to excel at the sport. He was also pleasantly surprised to discover Ernesto was an avid reader like himself. In fact, Alberto and Tomás found it diffi cult to believe that the young teenager Ernesto had already read so many books. Moreover, his reading list included the works of preeminent authors such as Sigmund Freud, Charles-Pierre Baudelaire, Émile Zola, Jack London,

Pablo Neruda, Anatole France, William Faulkner, John Steinbeck, and Karl Marx. He especially liked the poetry of Chile's famous poet Pablo Neruda, and his personal hero was Mahatma Gandhi, whom he deeply admired (Taibo:26).

Hilda Gadea (his fi rst wife) remembers that Ernesto told her he read everything in his father's library when he was teenager:

Ernesto told me how when he was still in high school he decided to start reading seriously and began by swallowing his father's library, choosing volumes at random. The books were not classifi ed and next to an adventure book he would fi nd a Greek tragedy and then a book on Marxism. (Gadea 2008:40)

H is interests were eclectic, but he took a special interest in poetry and could recite many of his favorite poems from memory. Although he read books on political topics and enjoyed discussing politics with his family and friends, most of his schoolmates remember him as being for the most part "politically disinterested" during his secondary school years (Anderson:33).

A s for sex, he was defi nitely interested. In the mid-1940s in Argentina, good girls were expected to remain a virgin until they married and boys from the upper classes were expected by their families and the social norms of their class to respect the virginity of the girls they dated, especially if they were from their same social circles. For their fi rst sexual experiences, therefore, boys from Ernesto's class went to brothels or had sexual relations with girls from the lower classes—often the young maids who worked in their homes or the homes of their friends. In Ernesto's case, his fi rst sexual experience appears to have occurred with a young maid when he was 15.

A friend from Alta Gracia, Carlos "Calica" Ferrer, arranged a sexual liaison for him with a Ferrer family maid, a young woman called "La Negra" Cabrera. Unknown to Ernesto at the time, Calica and a few of his friends spied on him while he had sex with the young woman. The following is a brief account of Ernesto's sexual initiation with La Negra:

T hey observed that, while he conducted himself admirably on top of the pliant maid, he periodically interrupted his lovemaking to suck on his asthma inhaler. The spectacle soon had them in stitches and remained a source of amusement for years afterward. (Anderson:35)

A. ccording to his friends, Ernesto was not perturbed by their jokes about his fi rst experience in lovemaking and continued for some time thereafter to have sexual relations with La Negra.

B. y the time he graduated from secondary school, Ernesto had "de-veloped into an extremely attractive young man: slim and wideshouldered, with dark-brown hair, intense brown eyes, clear white skin, and a self-contained, easy confi dence that made him alluring to girls" (Anderson:36). y the time he was 17, he had developed a devil-maycare and eccentric attitude that was characterized by his contempt for formality and social decorum and a penchant for shocking his teachers and classmates with his unconventional comments and behavior. He also bragged about how infrequently he took a bath or changed his clothes, and as a result he earned the nickname among his friends of "El Chancho" (the Pig) for his unkempt appearance and reluctance to bathe. What most of his friends did not realize was that he often had asthma attacks when he took a bath or shower, especially if the water was cold (Taibo:27).

In general, his grades in secondary school refl ected his interests. He did best in the subjects that most interested him: literature, history, and philosophy; his grades were weak in mathematics and natural history because they didn't interest him; and they were poor in English and music (Taibo 1996:28). He had no ear for music, and he was a poor dancer because he couldn't follow the music. In 1945 he took a serious interest in philosophy and compiled a 165-page notebook that he called his philosophical dictionary (the fi rst of seven such notebooks that he produced over the next 10 years). It contained in alphabetical order his notes on the main ideas and biographies of the important thinkers he had read and quotations of their defi nitions of key concepts such as love, immortality, sexual morality, justice, faith, God, death, reason, neurosis, and paranoia (Taibo:28). It also contained his commentaries on these notes, which he often wrote in the margins.

Thanks largely to his mother Celia's "egalitarian informality," his home was "a fascinating human zoo" that was frequented by a diverse range of colorful people of all social classes, occupations, levels of education, and ages, who often ate there and sometimes stayed a week or a month at a time (Anderson:39). His mother presided over this mélange of adults, teenagers, and children while Ernesto's father came and went on his old motorbike named "La Pedorra" (the Farter). Ernesto

found it diffi cult to study or read in such a chaotic and distracting environment, so he got into the habit of closing himself in the bathroom where he would read for hours. During this period, his parents became estranged but continued to live under the same roof.

I n 1946, Ernesto graduated from secondary school. He and his friend Tomás Granado (Alberto's younger brother) made plans to study engineering the following year at the University of Buenos Aires, and in the meantime they obtained jobs working for the provincial public highways department after taking a special course for fi eld analysts. Ernesto was hired as a materials analyst and sent to the north to inspect the materials being used on the roads around Villa María, where he was given free lodging and the use of a vehicle (Anderson:40). While he was there he was confronted with the news of two tragedies: he learned his hero from boyhood, Mahatma Gandhi (the famous leader of India's national independence movement against British colonial rule), had been assassinated and his beloved grandmother Ana Isabel Guevara was terminally ill (Taibo 1996:29).

B efore he left Villa María, he wrote a prophetic poem about his own death and his personal struggle to overcome his frequent asthma attacks. The following is an extract from this free-verse poem:

T he bullets, what can the bullets do to me if my destiny is to die by drowning.

But I am going to overcome destiny.

Destiny can be overcome by willpower.

Die yes, but riddled with bullets, destroyed by bayonets, if not, no.

D rowned, no . . . a memory more lasting than my name is to fi ght, to die fi ghting. (quoted in Anderson:44)

As this extract from a poem he wrote in January 1947 reveals, Ernesto had a premonition that he would die fi ghting —"riddled with bullets"— rather than drowning (from his asthma). This poem was written 20 years before he died—riddled with bullets—in 1967.

A. uring his absence from Córdoba, his family moved to Buenos Aires. His father's business was doing poorly and the family was forced to sell their house in Córdoba and move into the apartment his grandmother Ana Isabel Guevara owned and lived in. By May 1947 his grandmother was on her deathbed, and Ernesto gave up his job in Villa María to be at her bedside. According to his father:

B. rnesto [was] desperate at seeing that his grandmother didn't eat [so] he tried with incredible patience to get her to eat food, entertaining her, and without leaving her side. And he remained there until [she] left this world. (quoted in Anderson:41)

H e was greatly affected by the death of his grandmother, with whom he had a special emotional attachment; his sister Celia had never seen her older brother so upset and grief-stricken. Many years later she observed that "it must have been one of the greatest sadnesses of his life" (Anderson:41).

Apparently, the painful death of his beloved grandmother and his personal interest in fi nding a cure for asthma led him to change his mind about pursuing a degree in engineering and to study medicine instead (Anderson:42; Taibo:29). Within a month of arriving in Buenos Aires, he enrolled in the Faculty of Medicine at the University of Buenos Aires. His family believed he made this decision to change careers because of the shock of his grandmother's painful death and his desire to pursue a career that would alleviate human suffering. But his choice of specialties and research interests in medicine suggested he was also motivated by a desire to fi nd a cure for asthma. Years later, he said he chose a career in medicine because "I dreamed of becoming a famous investigator . . . of working indefatigably to fi nd something that could be defi nitively placed at the disposition of humanity" (quoted in Anderson:42).

In addition to his studies at the university, he held a number of parttime jobs. The one he held the longest was in the clinic of Dr. Salvador Pisani, where he also received treatment for his asthma (Anderson: 43). Dr. Pisani gave him the opportunity to work as a research assistant in the laboratory of his clinic, specifi cally on the pioneering use of vaccinations and other innovative types of treatment for the allergies associated with asthma. Ernesto became so enthralled in this research that he decided to specialize in the treatment of allergies for his medical career. He became a fi xture of Dr. Pisani's clinic and his home, where the doctor's mother and sister prepared a special antiasthma diet for Ernesto and took care of him when he suffered severe asthma attacks.

What little spare time he had he devoted to rugby, chess, and travel. He registered for military service as required when he was 18, but he was given a medical deferment from military service because of his asthma. As for his political orientation at this stage of his life, he was a "progressive liberal" who avoided affi liation with any political organization (Anderson:50). His political views were nationalist, anti-imperialist, and anti-American, but he was quite critical of the Argentine Communist Party and its youth organization at the university for their sectarianism (intolerance of other political organizations and ideologies). While he was not a Marxist, he did already have a special interest in Marx's writings and in socialist thought. At this stage of his life he was an engaging and intelligent nonconformist—an oddball who most of his friends and acquaintances found diffi cult to categorize.

S ince he was not quite 18 when the national election was held that elected Juan Perón to the presidency of Argentina in 1946, he was not able to vote in this historic election, but like most other students of his generation, he did not support Perón. His views regarding Perón have been characterized as "a-Peronism" (Castañeda:30–35), meaning he did not care much one way or the other about Perón and his policies. However, he reportedly told the maids who worked for his family that they should vote for Perón since his policies would help their class. It is not clear what he thought of Argentina's popular female political fi gure during this period—the beautiful blond radio actress Evita who was Perón's controversial mistress until he married her a few months before his election to the presidency in 1946.

During the years Ernesto was a university student, Eva "Evita" Duarte Perón became the darling of Argentina's popular classes because of her charismatic populist speeches and her highly publicized personal crusade for labor and women's rights (EPHRF 1997). While her husband was president, she ran the Argentine federal government's ministries of labor and health; founded and led the Eva Perón Foundation, which provided charitable services to the poor (especially to the elderly, women, and children); and created and served as the president of the nation's fi rst mass women's organization, called the Peronist Women's Party. After her death from cancer in 1952, Evita—like Che Guevara later—became a powerful icon in the political culture of Argentina and Latin America. However, there is no evidence there was ever any personal or political connection between these two historic fi gures.

After living in his deceased mother's apartment for a year, Ernesto's father sold his maté plantation and gave the money to Celia to buy a modest home in Buenos Aires at the edge of the desirable Palermo district (Anderson:44 – 45). However, to make ends meet, the older children had to fi nd jobs. Despite the now obvious separation between his parents—his father slept on the sofa in the living room of the new house—Ernesto maintained his close and open relationship with both parents, his father fondly describing their relationship during this period as follows:

We joked with one another as if we were the same age. He teased me continuously. As soon as we found ourselves at the table in our house, he would goad me with arguments of a political character. . . . Ernesto, who at that time was twenty years old, surpassed me in this area, and we argued constantly. Those who overheard us might have thought we were fi ghting. Not at all. Deep down there existed a true camaraderie between us. (quoted in Anderson:45)

Although his relationship was one of camaraderie with his father, with his mother it was more attentive and considerate, especially after she was diagnosed with breast cancer and had a mastectomy in 1946 (Anderson:56–57). She presided over the household in Buenos Aires in much the same way she did in Córdoba and Alta Gracia—she showed a complete disregard for social decorum and housekeeping but generously offered informal hospitality to all manner of guests. There was very little furniture and few decorations in the house, books were everywhere, and the walls in the kitchen gave electrical shocks because of a chronic short circuit in the electrical wiring.

E. rnesto often went to his Aunt Beatriz's (and deceased grandmoth-er's) apartment to study, and his father went there often to sleep, because of the noise and people coming and going in the family's house. rnesto had a special relationship with his spinster aunt, who loved to mother him. She would prepare meals for him and, according to his father, his Aunt Beatriz "didn't sleep while Ernesto studied; she always had his maté ready to prepare for him and accompanied him when he took a break, and she did this all with the greatest of affection" (quoted in Anderson:46). She was quite conservative and proper, so Ernesto loved to scandalize her with his ideas and stories but always in an affectionate and respectful manner. According to a cousin who accompanied him frequently to his aunt's apartment, Ernesto secretly seduced her maid without their aunt knowing anything about it (Anderson:47).

F. rom this period of his life, there is a photograph of Ernesto with his classmates in one of the classrooms of the aculty of Medicine at the University of Buenos Aires. A careful examination of this photograph provides some clues to Ernesto's character, state of mind, and his relationships at the time. In the photograph 28 white-coated students stand in three rows on different levels behind a naked cadaver with an open chest cavity on a metal table in the foreground. A few of the students are smiling at the camera and the rest have assumed a serious professional look, but in the third row is one student who is looking open-eyed at the camera with a broad joking smile —it is Ernesto. All the men are wearing ties, except for Ernesto, who is wearing a white shirt—probably the one white nylon shirt he owned and which he called "La Semanera" (the Weekly One) because he wore it all the time and washed it once a week. There are only three women in the group photograph, one of whom is Berta "Tita" Infante, with whom Ernesto had a deep but platonic relationship. She is looking at the camera with an intense gaze.

T ita and Ernesto met in an anatomy course and became very close friends and confi dants. It appears she wanted more from the relationship than he did or at least more than he was willing to give at the time. What follows is her description of Ernesto:

B y his accent he was a provincial, by his appearance he was a beautiful and uninhibited young man. . . . A mixture of shyness and arrogance, maybe the audacity hid his profound intelligence

and insatiable desire to understand things and there at the bottom

[of his heart], an infi nite capacity to love. (quoted in Taibo:32)

T hey met often, studied together, and discussed their personal problems. Their friendship lasted beyond medical school, and he corresponded almost as frequently with her after he left Argentina as he did with his mother and Aunt Beatriz.

A s for Ernesto's own refl ection on this period of his life, years later he said the following:

W hen I began to study medicine, the majority of the concepts that I have as a revolutionary were absent from the storehouse of my ideas. I wanted to succeed, like everyone; I dreamed of being a famous researcher, dreamed of working untiringly to succeed at doing something that could be defi nitively placed at the disposal of humanity, but in that moment it was a personal achievement [that I wanted]. I was, as we all are, a child of my environment. (quoted in Taibo:32)

Thus, Che (the revolutionary), looking back on his student years, saw himself as a product of his own environment—someone who was primarily concerned with his own individual success and not yet someone who was prepared unselfi shly to place himself at the service of humanity.

CHAPTER THREE

Guevara's South American Odyssey

Ernesto loved to travel. His father wrote that with time he came to understand "his obsession with travelling was just another part of his zeal for learning" (Guevara 1995:2). However, Ernesto disguised this motivation for his early trips by talking casually about his travel plans and by at least pretending to be motivated primarily by the desire for adventure. His diary of his now famous 1951–1952 trip (Guevara 1995) throughout South America is written primarily in this vein. However, his subsequent 1953–1954 trip throughout South and Central America was clearly motivated by more serious intentions, especially after he reached Central America (see chapter 3).

A. rnesto's fi rst noteworthy journey on his own took place in 1950, when he toured all of central and northern Argentina by motorbike—a trip of some 4,000 miles (Gambini 1968:22). He was 21 and a medical student at the University of Buenos Aires at the time. On his journey he stopped off in Córdoba to visit his friends Tomás and Alberto Granado. Alberto was conducting research on lepers at a leprosarium near San Francisco del Chañar, and because rnesto was intrigued by Alberto's research he spent several days with Alberto at the leprosarium.

B. rom there he headed north and met an interesting assortment of hobos, vagabonds, seasonal workers, poor indigenous inhabitants, and other socially marginalized people along the way. He often stayed overnight in police stations and provincial hospitals where he asked if he could sleep in vacant jail cells or empty hospital beds. As a result, "for the fi rst time in his adult life, Ernesto . . . witnessed the harsh duality of his country by crossing the divide from its transported European culture, which was also *his* [culture], and . . . its ignored, backward, *indigenous* heartland" (Anderson 1997:63).

W hat he learned from this trip to the poorer northern region of his country was that Argentina's more modern and superfi cial European culture was "a luxurious façade under which the country's true soul lay; and that soul was rotten and diseased." It was from this region of the country that "the Argentine Indians, commonly referred to as *coyas,* and the mixed-blood *cabezitas negras* (little black heads) fl ed in steadily increasing numbers, pouring into the cities in search of work and setting up shantytowns like the one in front of the Guevaras' home in Córdoba" (Anderson 1997:64). They were the social class of domestic servants and day laborers called *descamisados* (shirtless ones) whom Péron and his wife Evita promised to incorporate into the nation and whom Argentina's white elite still exploit and despise.

W hen Ernesto returned to Buenos Aires from this trip he took the motorbike back to the store where he bought it in order to have it reconditioned. When the store owner discovered the details of the trip, he was astounded and asked Ernesto to give him a letter attesting to his having made such a fantastic trip using the particular brand of motorbike that he used. This letter, along with a picture of Ernesto sitting on his motorbike, was published in a local sports magazine as an advertisement for this type of motorbike (Taibo 1996:35).

E rnesto returned to his studies in medical school, resumed playing rugby, and continued working in Dr. Pisani's clinic. He also fell in love for the fi rst time. The object of his affection was the 16-year-old daughter of one of Córdoba's wealthiest families. Her name was María del Carmen "Chichina" Ferreyra, and they met in October 1950 at a wedding in Córdoba attended by Ernesto and his family. By all accounts, she was a strikingly beautiful, intelligent, and charming young woman, who was as infatuated with him as he was with her (Taibo:37). However, this romance was doomed from the start since Chichina was a pampered young princess from the "blue-blooded Argentina gentry, heiress to the Ferreyra family empire," while Ernesto was the Bohemian prodigal son of "a family of pauperized aristocrats" who after generations of decline were at best precarious members of Argentina's upper middle class (Anderson 1997:65).

Chichina's family lived in an imposing French-style chateau with parklike gardens in Córdoba and on a large estate called La Malagueño outside of the city. According to her cousin, Dolores Moyano:

[This estate] included two polo fi elds, Arabian stallions, and a feudal village of workers for the family's limestone quarries. The family visited the village church every Sunday for Mass, worshipping in a separate alcove to the right of the altar with its own separate entrance and private communion rail, away from the mass of workers. In many ways, La Malagueño exemplifi ed everything that Ernesto despised. Yet, unpredictable as always, Ernesto had fallen madly in love with the princess of this little empire, my cousin Chichina Ferreyra, an extraordinarily beautiful and charming girl, who, to the dismay of her parents, was equally fascinated by Ernesto. (quoted in Anderson:65)

Ernesto became a frequent, if not always welcome, visitor at the Ferreyras' homes in Córdoba and at La Malagueño.

E rnesto was madly in love with Chichina and wanted to marry her. But the differences in their age and social class, her parents' disapproval of him, and the distance between them began to strain their relationship. At the beginning of 1951, Ernesto needed to earn some money, so he signed up to serve as a ship's nurse on Argentina's merchant marine freighters and oil tankers (Taibo:38). Between February and June 1951, he made various trips back and forth between Argentina and Brazil, Venezuela, and the Caribbean islands. These trips gave him plenty of time to study for his medical exams and exposed him to life at sea as well as most of the ports of call on the Atlantic Coast of South America and in the Caribbean. At the end of June 1951, he went back to medical school.

On one of his visits to Córdoba to see Chichina he also visited his friends the Granado brothers. In the course of a conversation with Alberto Granado while working on his motorcycle, nicknamed La Poderosa (the Powerful One), the idea of making a yearlong trip together took shape. Ernesto's account of this momentous occasion is as follows:

Our fantasizing took us to far away places, sailing tropical seas, travelling through Asia. And suddenly, slipping in as if part of our fantasy, came the question:

"Why don't we go to North America? " "North America? How? " "On La Poderosa, man." That's how the trip came about, and it never deviated from the general principle laid down then: improvisation. . . . My task before leaving was to take as many exams in as many subjects as possible; Alberto's to get the bike ready for the long journey. . . . At that stage the momentousness of our endeavor hadn't dawned on us, all we could see was the dusty road ahead and us on our bike devouring kilometers in the fl ight northward. (Guevara 1995:13)

They were both restless and anxious to set out on an adventure. Alberto had quit his job, and Ernesto was tired of medical school, hospitals, and studying for exams. He was also frustrated by the opposition of Chichina's parents to their relationship. For these reasons, they both wanted to take a break from their existing circumstances.

Thus, in December 1951, when he lacked only one year of receiving his medical degree, Ernesto and his friend Alberto Granados decided to set out to explore all of Latin America by motorcycle. Ernesto's *Motorcycle Diaries* (Guevara 1995), which were published many years after his death, provide a valuable personal narrative of this journey. They shed light on a little known period in his young adulthood and provide important insights into his personality and the development of his views about the world. Written while he was traveling around South America in his early 20s, they allow the reader to gain an intimate portrait of him at an important and formative period in his life. Ironically, most of this trip was not made on a motorcycle. In fact, Ernesto and Alberto traveled on just about every mode of transportation available at the time—horses, railroads, buses, trucks, cars, ships, ferries, boats, rafts, and airplanes— and of course on their feet.

After their motorcycle died in Chile, they were forced to walk, hitchhike, and use whatever means was available to make their way from one end of the South American continent to the other.

Ernesto's lucid and brief accounts in his diary enable the reader to almost hear his thoughts, view the world through his eyes, and sense his spirit. In a certain sense they allow the reader to travel back in time to meet the man before he made his grand entrance on the stage of world history as one of the most charismatic and emblematic revolutionaries of all time.

From Buenos Aires, Ernesto and Alberto traveled to the Atlantic Coast of Argentina and across the pampa to the south of Argentina, where they crossed the Andes Mountains into Chile. They had increasing problems with the motorcycle as they traveled over the Andes and through southern Chile. As they neared the Chilean capital of Santiago, the motorcycle fi nally gave out and they had to continue the rest of their trip on foot. They also quickly ran out of money. They were forced to panhandle, freeload, and work at numerous odd jobs in order to continue their journey northward through Chile to Peru, through Peru to Colombia, and fi nally to Venezuela. Along the way, Ernesto developed a critical social consciousness based on the many instances of social injustice, human exploitation, and racial and ethnic discrimination he witnessed in all the countries he visited. He also developed a Latin American identity as he discovered that the people in these countries shared common values, aspirations, and sociohistorical conditions.

When Ernesto announced his travel plans to his family they were surprised to learn he planned to be away for a whole year, particularly because of his love affair with

Chichina (Guevara 1995:1). When his father asked him about her, Ernesto said: "If she loves me, she'll wait." Years later, his father refl ected on Ernesto's motivations for this trip in the prologue he wrote for the so-called *Motorcycle Diaries*. He said he really did not understand his son's motivations at the time and it was only many years later that he realized what truly motivated him. He wrote:

I was puzzled. I didn't understand Ernesto. There were things about him I couldn't quite fathom. They only became clear with time. I didn't realize then that his obsession with travelling was just another part of his zeal for learning. He knew that really to understand the needs of the poor he had to travel the world, not as a tourist stopping to take pretty pictures and enjoy the scenery, but . . . by sharing the human suffering found at every bend in the road. . . . Years later, thinking back over his continuous travelling, I realized that it had convinced him of his true destiny. (Guevara 1995:2)

His father also noted that he was fooled by the very casual manner in which his son talked about his trips, mistakenly assuming he was primarily motivated by curiosity and adventure. However, through reading his letters and later his diaries, his father realized his son "was following a true missionary impulse which never left him" and possessed a "mystical and certain knowledge of his own destiny" (Guevara 1995:3–4). The choice of the term "missionary" is somewhat misleading, since Ernesto at this stage was certainly not concerned with propagating a specifi c ideology or doctrine. He was very open-minded, quite secular in his thinking, and generally respectful of the cultural differences he encountered in his travels. In fact, there is very little evidence of the kind of dogmatism and ethnocentrism in his thinking that one associates with the thinking of most missionaries.

His father had to suffer in silence the fears he had for his son when he learned he was planning to take a year away from his studies to go on the incredible transcontinental odyssey he and his friend Alberto Granado had planned. According to his father:

When he told me of the journey he planned with Granado, I took him aside and said: "You've some hard times ahead. How can I advise against it when it's something I've always dreamed of myself? But remember, if you get lost in those jungles and I don't hear from you at reasonable intervals, I'll come looking for you, trace your steps, and won't come back until I fi nd you." (Guevara 1995:3)

In response, Ernesto promised his father he would write frequently and keep him informed of his route of travel, which he faithfully did.

He and Alberto started out on their journey on January 4, 1952— midsummer in the Southern Hemisphere. They went fi rst to the Atlantic Coast of Argentina to visit one of Ernesto's uncles in Villa Gisell and then to the beach resort city of Miramar to say good-bye to Chichina, who was vacationing there with one of her aunts. Ernesto brought with him a puppy for Chichina whom he signifi cantly named "Come Back." He ended up staying eight days in Miramar, and Alberto was worried he was going to change his mind about going ahead with their trip.

E rnesto wrote the following in his diary about this romantic interlude at the outset of their long journey:

The trip hung in the balance, in a cocoon, subordinate to the word which consents and ties. Alberto saw the danger and was already imagining himself alone on the highways and byways of America, but he said nothing. The tug of war was between her and me. . . . The two days I'd planned stretched like elastic into eight and with the bittersweet taste of goodbye mingling with my inveterate halitosis I fi nally felt myself wafted away on the winds of adventure. (Guevara 1995:17)

In Miramar, he tried to obtain both Chichina's promise to wait for him and her gold bracelet as a keepsake to take with him on the trip. She didn't give him either, but she did give him $15 to purchase a scarf for her in the United States (the planned end point of their journey).

S. everal weeks later in the Andean mountain resort of Bariloche, Er-nesto found a letter from Chichina waiting for him at the local post offi ce, where they had previously arranged he would pick up his mail. In this letter, she informed him she had decided not to wait for him. In his diary, he wrote the following about his reactions: "I read and re-read the incredible letter. uddenly all my dreams of home, bound up with the eyes which saw me off in Miramar, were shattered, apparently for no good reason" (page 35). Although he was clearly hurt and wanted at fi rst to write "a weepy letter," he realized it was hopeless to convince her to change her mind. He also wrote: "I thought I loved her until this moment when I realized I couldn't feel, I had to think her back again."

T. he next day Ernesto and Alberto crossed a mountain lake into Chile on a leaking ferry boat that they kept afl oat by pumping out the bilge water in return for their free passage. On this boat they met some Chilean doctors who told them there was a leper colony on Easter Island (Rapa Nui, or Isla de Pascua), some 2,000 miles from mainland Chile in the southeastern Pacifi

c. As Ernesto wrote in his diary: "It was a wonderful island, they said, and our scientifi c appetites were whetted" (page 37). hey resolved to travel to the island and asked one of the doctors to give them a letter of introduction to the president of the Friends of Easter Island in Valparaíso, where they hoped they could secure passage on a ship going to the island.

With their money running low, they were forced to freeload their way through southern Chile. In the southern port city of Valdivia they dropped in on the local newspaper, which interviewed them for an article about their journey. As a result, they decided in a gesture of great magnanimity to dedicate their trip to the city since it was celebrating the 400th anniversary of its founding. At their next stop, in the picturesque central Chilean town of Temuco, they were interviewed again by the local newspaper, which was printed under the title: "Two Argentine Leprology Experts Tour South America by Motorbike" (page 40).

Ernesto's account in his diary of this article and their short stay in Temuco reveals some of the fl avor of their trip at this point as well as his tongue-in-cheek view of their freeloading style of travel. He wrote:

We had asked permission to leave the bike in the garage of a man who lived on the outskirts and we now made our way there, no longer just a pair of reasonably likeable bums with a bike in tow. No, we were now "the experts," and that's how we were treated. We spent the day fi xing the bike and a little dark maid kept coming up with edible treats. At fi ve o'clock, after a sumptuous "snack" laid on by our host, we said goodbye to Temuco and headed north. (page 40)

They didn't get very far before they noticed their back tire had a puncture that they couldn't fi x. They were worried they would have to spend the night in the open, but as Ernesto recounts in his diary: "We weren't just anybody now, we were the experts; we soon found a railway worker who took us to his house where we were treated like kings" (page 41).

They fi xed the tire at a garage the next day and resumed their trip, but they soon encountered more trouble. Without any warning, their motorcycle veered sideways and threw them off. The crash broke the bike's steering column and smashed its gearbox. This was the beginning of the end of La Poderosa. Although they managed to weld the steering column and fi x the gearbox at a local garage, the bike was never the same again.

While they were working on the bike at this garage they bummed something to eat and drink at the homes of the curiosity seekers who dropped by to see the two famous travelers working on their motorcycle.

Their last night in Temuco they were invited by the mechanics at the garage to have drinks with them and go to a village dance, where Ernesto got drunk and caused an altercation on the dance fl oor. He wrote the following account of this incident in his diary:

Chilean wine is very good and I was downing it at an amazing rate, so by the time we went on to the village dance I felt ready for anything. . . . One of the mechanics from the garage, a particularly nice guy, asked me to dance with his wife because he'd been mixing his drinks and was the worse for wear. His wife was pretty randy [feeling horny] and obviously in the mood, and I, full of Chilean wine, took her by the hand to lead her outside. She followed me docilely but then realized her husband was watching and changed her mind. I was in no state to listen to reason and we had a bit of a barney [quarrel] in the middle of the dance fl oor, resulting in me pulling her toward one of the doors with everybody watching. She tried to kick me and as I was pulling her she lost her balance and went crashing to the fl oor. (page 42)

He and Alberto had to quickly leave the scene, "pursued by a swarm of enraged dancers." Since they had now worn out the hospitality of their local hosts, they left the next day, but only after having lunch at the house of the family that lived next to the garage.

O n the road north to Santiago, they had another bad spill on the motorcycle and they had to repair it once again. Shortly thereafter, the bike fi nally gave its last gasp going up a steep hill, and they had to hitch a lift on a truck going to the town of Los Angeles. They arranged to stay in a volunteer fi re station in Los Angeles and in a few days found a truck to take them and the bike to Santiago, where they left the corpse of La Poderosa at a garage. At this point in their journey Ernesto noted they ceased being "motorized bums" and became "non-motorized bums" (page 44).

From this point forward they had to rely on their freeloading skills to hitch rides, bum meals and lodgings, work at odd jobs when they could, and panhandle their way northward to Peru. Ernesto noted in his diary their transition to this new stage in their journey:

We were used to attracting idle attention with our strange garb and the prosaic fi gure of La Poderosa II, whose asthmatic wheezing aroused pity in our hosts. All the same, we had been, so to speak, gentlemen of the road. We'd belonged to a time-honored aristocracy of wayfarers, bearing our degrees as visiting cards to impress people. Not any more. Now we were just two tramps with packs on our backs, and the grime of the road encrusted in our overalls, shadows of our former aristocratic selves. (page 49)

They went from Santiago to Valparaíso only to discover there were no ships leaving from this port city to go to Easter Island for another six months.

While they were in Valparaíso they made friends with the owner of a bar named La Gioconda (the name of a famous Italian opera and another name for the Mona Lisa painting). The bar owner would not let them pay for their food or drink and even let them sleep in the kitchen. He was found of saying: "Today it's your turn, tomorrow it'll be mine" (page 51). While they were there, he asked Ernesto to visit one of his elderly customers who was suffering from asthma and a bad heart.

E. rnesto's comments in his diary about this old woman reveal a great deal about his social views at this stage in his life. He observed that "the poor thing was in an awful state, breathing the smell of stale sweat and dirty feet that fi lled her room, mixed with the dust from a couple of armchairs," which were "the only luxuries in her house" (page 52). Such circumstances, he said, made a doctor feel powerless and long for change that would end the social injustices of the present order. He noted that in such cases "we see the profound tragedy which circumscribes the life of the proletariat [working class] the world over," since the poverty of their existence makes them at the end of their lives a bitter burden for the poor family members who have to take care of them. His concluding comments were these: "How long this present order, based on an absurd idea of caste, will last I can't say," but he added it was time for governments to spend "more money, much more money, funding socially useful projects."

F. rom Valparaíso, Ernesto and Alberto stowed away on a boat that was headed for the northern port of Antofagasta. They were discovered after the boat was at sea and forced to do menial chores such as cleaning the latrines and the decks. However, at night the captain invited them to drink and play cards with him. When they arrived in Antofagasta they tried to stow away on another boat headed farther north, but they were caught before it sailed and put onshore. Instead, they traveled north overland through the desert by hitching rides on trucks. So it was that they ended up visiting Chile's largest copper mine at Chuquicamata.

O n the way they made friends with a married couple who were mine workers and members of the Chilean Communist Party. The husband told them about his three months in prison as a result of the Chilean government's proscription of the party and persecution of its members, and about "his starving wife who followed him with exemplary loyalty, his children left in the care of a kindly neighbor, his fruitless pilgrimage in search of work and his comrades who had mysteriously disappeared and were said to be somewhere at the bottom of the sea" (page 59). According to his diary, when Ernesto and Alberto encountered the couple, they were "numb with cold, huddling together in the desert night" without "a single miserable blanket to sleep under, so we gave them one of ours and Alberto and I wrapped the other around us as best we could."

Ernesto saw them as "a living symbol of the proletariat the world over" and wrote that "it's really upsetting to think they use repressive measures against people like these," since what motivated them to join the Communist Party was "nothing more than the natural desire for a better life" and their "protest against persistent hunger." He observed that this motivation had led them to adopt Communist ideology, whose real meaning he felt they could never grasp, but when it was translated into "bread for the poor" was something that they could understand and that gave them hope for the future (page 60).

W hen he and Alberto visited the huge U.S.-owned, open-pit copper mine at Chuquicamata, they were offended by the condescending manner of the U.S. managers and the hazardous working conditions and poor pay of the Chilean mine workers. In his diary, he wrote: "The bosses, the blond, effi cient, arrogant managers, told us in primitive Spanish: 'this isn't a tourist town. I'll get a guide to give you a half-hour tour around the mine and then please be good enough to leave, we have a lot of work to do' " (page 60). He also noted that a strike was being planned at the mine and wrote in his diary that their guide, who he called "the Yankee bosses' faithful lapdog, told us: 'Stupid gringos, they lose thousands of pesos every day in a strike so as not to give a poor worker a couple of extra centavos.' "

Ernesto noted in his diary that "Chile offers economic possibilities to anyone willing to work as long as he's not from the proletariat," since the country had enough mineral resources (copper, iron, coal, tin, gold, silver, manganese, nitrates, etc.) to make it an industrial power. However, he observed that "the main thing Chile has to do is to get its tiresome Yankee friend off its back, a Herculean task, at least for the time being, given the huge US investment and the ease with which it can bring economic pressure to bear whenever its interests are threatened" (page 71).

From Chuquicamata, Ernesto and Alberto hitchhiked to the Peruvian border. I n Peru, they adopted a pattern of hitching rides on the trucks carrying people and freight between the main towns and asking if they could stay overnight in the guard stations of the Peruvian Civil Guard (the country's paramilitary national police force) or the hospitals in the towns where they stopped. As they traveled, they came in close contact with Peru's exploited and suffering Indian masses, who represent a majority of the population. They saw how the Indians of the Peruvian altiplano (high plateau) were (and still are) exploited and oppressed.

In Tarata, Peru, Ernesto wrote in his diary about how the local Peruvian Indians (the Aymarás) "are not the same proud race that time after time rose up against Inca rule and forced them to maintain a permanent army on their borders"; rather, they had become "a defeated race" since the Spanish Conquest and centuries of colonial domination. He noted that "they look at us meekly, almost fearfully, completely indifferent to the outside world," and "some give the impression that they go on living simply because it's a habit they can't give up" (page 77).

A. fter they left Tarata, they traveled on the same truck with a school-teacher who had been fi red by the government because he was a member of the leftist PRA party (American Popular Revolutionary Alliance). He was part Indian and seemed to know a great deal about Peru's indigenous cultures and customs. He told Ernesto and Alberto about the animosity that exists between the Indians, whom he admired, and the mestizos (half-bloods), whom he considered "wily and cowardly," even though he was technically one himself. According to

Ernesto: "The teacher's voice took on a strange inspired resonance whenever he spoke about his Indians . . . and it switched to deep despondency when he spoke of the Indians' present conditions, brutalized by modern civilization and the impure mestizos" (page 81).

The teacher told Ernesto and Alberto about the need to establish schools for the Indians that would teach them to "value their own world" and that would "enable them to play a useful role within it." He also spoke about "the need to change completely the present system of education," which he said "on the rare occasions it does offer Indians an education (education, that is, according to the white man's criteria), only fi lls them with shame and resentment, leaving them unable to help their fellow Indians and at a tremendous disadvantage in a white society which is hostile to them" (page 81).

Ernesto made frequent references in his diary to the plight of the Indians and to the injustices and discrimination they suffered at the hands of the whites and mestizos. When he and Alberto visited the magnifi cent Incan ruins of Machu Picchu, he also noted how the North American tourists paid little or no attention to how the Indians lived. Although he and Alberto traveled to the ruins on the third-class train used only by the local Indians, he observed: "The tourists travelling in their comfortable railcars can only have the very vaguest idea of how the Indians live, gleaned from a quick glance as they whizz by our train which has to stop to let them pass" (page 101). And he later criticized how the wealthier people in Peru expected their Indian servants "to carry anything heavy and put up with any discomfort" (page 108).

B. ecause of their interest in leprosy, they went to Lima, the capital city of Peru, to meet Dr. Hugo Pesce, a well-known expert in leprology and a university professor. Dr. Pesce put them up in the leper hospital he ran in Lima and invited them to eat dinner at his house, which they did just about every night while they stayed in Lima. They divided their time between the leper hospital and the National Museum of the Archaeology, Anthropology, and History of Peru, which presents the history of Peru from prehistoric times to the colonial era.

Ernesto also had long conversations about philosophy, politics, and critical health issues in Latin America with Dr. Pesce, who was a disciple of the Peruvian Marxist philosopher José Carlos Mariátegui and a prominent member of the Peruvian Communist Party. Pesce had been forced into political exile during the fi rst years of the dictatorship of General Manuel Odría (1948–1956) and was probably the fi rst man of medicine Ernesto and Alberto had met who was genuinely living a highly principled life and totally dedicated to serving the common good (Anderson 1997:85–86).

In Lima, Ernesto and Alberto decided to give up their original objective of traveling to the United States. They chose Venezuela as their ultimate destination after fi rst visiting Dr. Pesce's largest treatment center for lepers in Peru's Amazonian region. When they were ready to leave, the patients of the leper hospital in Lima gave them an emotional send-off party. They were very touched by the affectionate farewell the patients gave them and by the small collection of money they presented them for their trip. Ernesto wrote in his diary that "some had tears in their eyes as they thanked us for coming, spending time with them, accepting their presents, sitting listening to football [soccer] on the radio with them," and he added that "if anything were to make us seriously specialize in leprosy, it would be the affection the patients show us wherever we go" (page 123).

S omewhat later, in a letter he wrote to his father from Iquitos, Peru, he observed that "their appreciation stemmed from the fact that we didn't wear overalls or gloves, that we shook hands with them as we would the next man, sat with them chatting about this and that, and played football with them." He added: "This may seem pointless bravado, but the psychological benefi t to these people—usually treated like animals—of being treated as normal human beings is incalculable and the risk incredibly remote" (page 132).

Their destination when they set out from Lima was the San Pablo leper colony situated on the banks of the Amazon River. They hitchhiked from Lima to Pucallpa and then took a boat down the Ucayali River (one of the headwaters of the Amazon) to Iquitos. From Iquitos they took another boat down the Amazon to the San Pablo leper colony. Once there, they volunteered to work in the leprosarium's laboratory and endeared themselves to both the staff and the patients. They played soccer with the patients, took them on hikes, and even led them on hunting expeditions.

While they were at the colony, Ernesto turned 24 and the staff threw a birthday party for him. After he was given a touching toast by the director of the colony, Ernesto replied to the toast as expected under such circumstances. An excerpt from his account of this speech is worth quoting since it reveals his newfound Latin American identity and also what would become one of his deepest political convictions:

I n a few days we will be leaving Peru, so these words are also a farewell, and I'd like to stress my gratitude to all the people of this country, who over and over again since we arrived . . . have shown us the warmth of their hospitality. And I would like to add another thought, nothing to do with this toast. Although we're too insignifi cant to be spokesmen for such a noble cause, we believe, and this journey has only served to confi rm this belief, that the division of America into unstable and illusory nations is a complete fi ction. We are one single mestizo race with remarkable ethnographical similarities, from Mexico down to the Magellan Straits. And so, in an attempt to break free from all narrow-minded provincialism, I propose a toast to Peru and to a United America. (page 135)

T he speech received loud applause, and one can see in it the stirrings of his political oratory skills as well as his ultimate political mission—the political unifi cation of Latin America.

When it came time for Ernesto and Alberto to leave, some of the patients gave them a very emotional farewell serenade, with a blind man singing local songs and a man with virtually no fi ngers playing an accordion. Alberto thanked them and said they were both deeply touched. The next day, Ernesto and Alberto went to see the patients and after taking some photographs with them came back with two large pineapples. After saying their fi nal good-byes they cast off in a raft, named Mambo-Tango, built for them by one of the staff members so they could go down the river to Leticia, Colombia, where the borders of Colombia, Peru, and Brazil meet on the upper Amazon.

I n Leticia, they got 50 percent off on the weekly fl ight to Bogotá and made some money coaching and playing for the town's soccer team. When they arrived in Bogotá they obtained permission to stay at a hospital where they were offered jobs in the leprosy service. However, they had a run-in with the local police over a knife Ernesto carried with him that was a present from his brother Roberto. They were harassed so badly by the police they decided to leave for Venezuela as soon as possible.

In reference to this encounter with the Colombian police in a letter Ernesto wrote to his mother from Bogotá, he observed: "There is more repression of individual freedom here than in any country we've been to, the police patrol the streets carrying rifl es and demand your papers every few minutes, which some of them read upside down" (page 144). He also wrote that "the countryside is in open revolt and the army is powerless to put it down." Because of this situation, he said: "We're getting out of here as soon as we can." A few days later, the two harassed travelers left Bogotá on a bus headed for Venezuela.

They made their way to Caracas, the capital of Venezuela. Alberto looked up a doctor who was a specialist in leprology. Impressed by Alberto's interest in leprosy, the doctor offered him a position in his laboratory. At about the same time, Ernesto ran into an uncle who had an airplane that he used to transport race horses between Buenos Aires and Miami. The uncle told Ernesto that he could return with him to Buenos Aires if he wanted to resume his studies at medical school. Ernesto and Alberto made a pact: Alberto would accept the job offered him and stay in Venezuela, while Ernesto would go back to Buenos Aires to graduate from medical school and then return to Venezuela to work with Alberto. It was the end of July 1952 when they said good-bye in Caracas.

In one of the last entries in his diary, Ernesto commented on how much he missed Alberto. He said: "I'm always turning around to tell him something and then I realize he's not there." And he added: "All these months we've been together through thick and thin and the habit of dreaming the same dreams in similar situations has made us even closer." On the other hand, the same entry makes it clear he was looking forward to "going home to start my studies again and fi nally getting the degree which will enable me to practice [medicine]" (page 148).

When Ernesto left Caracas, the plane he took went to Miami, where it was scheduled to stop before returning to Buenos Aires. However, when they got to Miami the plane had mechanical problems, so it had to be repaired before it could leave for Buenos Aires. Ernesto took advantage of this opportunity to get to know the city (pages 153–54). As it turned out, he had to wait a whole month for the plane to be repaired. He had no money, but he was able to stay in a small hotel by promising to pay the bill from Buenos Aires as soon as he returned, which he did. During the month that he stayed in Miami, Ernesto visited the beaches and hung around with an Argentine student he met, who helped him fi nd a job as a dishwasher in one of Miami's restaurants. When the plane was repaired, he fl ew back to Buenos Aires. It was September 1952.

In the prologue he wrote for Ernesto's *The Motorcycle Diaries,* his father says we can see in this written account of Ernesto's eight-month journey that he "had faith in himself as well as the will to succeed, and a tremendous determination to achieve what he set out to do" (page 4). He also recounts the observations made about Ernesto by a priest, Father Cuchetti, a friend of the family who was well known in Argentina for his liberal views. When he told him about Ernesto and Alberto's trip to the Amazon and their stay in the San Pablo leper colony, the priest said the following: "I take my hat off to your son and his friend's humanity and integrity, because to do what [they did] takes more than just guts: you need a will of iron and an enormously compassionate and charitable soul. Your son will go far" (page 2).

The Motorcycle Diaries reveal Ernesto's growing political consciousness and his early leanings toward socialism as he learned fi rsthand during his travels of the extreme conditions of social injustice and oppression that prevail throughout Latin America. However, what is most striking about *The Motorcycle Diaries* is that while they reveal he had a strong desire to help others less fortunate than himself, he did not possess the kind of self-righteousness or exaggerated piety that one often associates with zealous do-gooders and missionaries.

T he legendary actor, producer, and director Robert Redford produced a popular fi lm version of *The Motorcycle Diaries,* which was directed by the well-known Brazilian fi lm director Walter Salles. The fi lm was shown in cinemas around the world during 2004 and 2005. It provides a moving account of Ernesto's journey with his friend Alberto Granado throughout Latin America. It stars the popular Mexican actor Gael García Bernal as the young Ernesto, while Alberto is played by the Argentine actor Rodrigo de la Serna, who is related to Ernesto "Che" Guevara through his mother's side of the family. After making the fi lm, García Bernal reportedly said: "He's a person that changed the world and he has really forced me to change the rules of what I am" (Osborne 2003).

Redford traveled to Havana to obtain permission to make the fi lm from Che's widow, Aleida March, who maintains an archive of all his writings, offi cial papers, and information written about him. When the production of the fi lm was completed, Redford returned to Cuba to host a special screening, which was attended by Aleida, 84-year-old Alberto Granado, Che's sons and daughters, his former comrades, and people who had worked closely with him during the early years of the Cuban revolution. According to Redford, the fi lm was well received by this audience, and he said later: "I could have probably died there in the seat. When I heard people sniffi ng and crying and I thought either they're so upset with me I'm not gonna get out of here, or they liked the fi lm, which they did" (Smiley 2004).

T he fi lm was generally well received by critics and won various awards, including one Oscar. It was not widely distributed in the United States and earned only some $16 million in the United States, while it earned over $40 million at cinemas in other parts of the world. Gael García Bernal criticized the poor distribution of the fi lm in the United States. According to the Internet Movie Database (IMDb), García Bernal told an interviewer for the *Detroit Free Press* that the Hollywood studio system relegates pictures like *The Motorcycle Diaries* to limited screenings in art fi lm theatres. As a result, most people in the United States never even consider seeing them and they do not get the chance to compete with the well-funded, mainstream Hollywood fi lms. He said: "They get tossed off as foreign and independent fi lms like they are somehow not ready to compete with all that crap that Hollywood produces." Nevertheless, the fi lm is available in DVD format and can be purchased or rented.

As his diaries and the fi lm reveals, Ernesto learned a great deal about Latin America and himself through his travels. As a young man wandering around South America, he learned to take pleasure in traveling for days on end with little or no money, without the possibility of taking a bath and changing his clothes, and not even knowing when he would eat next or where he would stay the night. The knowledge he gained from this experience of surviving on his own wits and the personal traits he developed as a result of traveling from day to day in this manner helped prepare him for the life he would lead much later as a guerrilla fi ghter, when he often had to survive without food, water, bathing, or adequate clothing.

CHAPTER FOUR

A Call to arms in Guatemala and Mexico

A fter he returned to Argentina, Ernesto undertook the remaining courses and exams to complete the requirements for his graduation from medical school. He met all the remaining requirements in less than a year and obtained his medical degree in March 1953. He still wanted to join Alberto Granado in Caracas as they had planned at the end of their trip together in July 1952, and he wanted at some point to visit Europe and maybe Asia. He did not want to settle down to a comfortable bourgeois life as a well-paid doctor in Argentina. Thus, at 25 years old with his medical degree in hand, Ernesto decided to set out on his second Latin American odyssey.

As his old friend Alberto Granado states in the foreword to the published version, *Back on the Road* (*Otra Vez*), of the diary Ernesto kept during this trip (Guevara 2001:vii):

Whereas his fi rst trip in South America served to deepen his ideas about social distinctions and made him see the importance of struggling against them, this second journey consolidates the political knowledge he has acquired and fuels a growing need for further study to grasp why and how a struggle must be waged that will culminate in a genuine revolution.

His old friend is absolutely correct when he observes that while Ernesto is still motivated by a desire for travel and the study of archeology (particularly the Incan, Mayan, and Aztec civilizations), his political views were increasingly radicalized by the political, economic, and social conditions he witnessed in the countries he visited, especially Guatemala.

O n this trip he is accompanied by another childhood friend, Carlos "Calica" Ferrer, whose political awareness, interests, and temperament are less compatible with those of Ernesto than were those of Alberto. While he starts the trip with a vague plan to join Alberto in Caracas and has some notion of later traveling to Europe and maybe Asia, he changes his travel plans in Ecuador, goes from there to Guatemala, and ends up in Mexico two years later. As Ricardo Gott notes in the introduction to Ernesto's diary of this trip (Guevara 2001:xv), the experiences he has in this lengthy journey change him from "a detached and cynical observer" to "a fully fl edged revolutionary, seeking a theoretical framework through which to understand the world, and ardent in his desire to take immediate action to change it."

O n July 7, 1953, Ernesto and Calica set out on the fi rst leg of their journey—the 1,600-mile train trip from Buenos Aires to La Paz, Bolivia. As Ricardo Gott writes in *Back on the Road* (Guevara 2001:xiii): "His mother and father would not see him again for another six years," and "by that time their itinerate son had become famous throughout the world as 'Che' Guevara, the guerrilla fi ghter who had fought alongside Fidel Castro to bring revolutionary change to Cuba." And it would be another eight years (in 1961) before he would visit his homeland again, as one of the most important leaders of the new revolutionary government of Cuba. His outlook at the start of the trip is that of a Latin American (not just an Argentine), but by the time he visits Argentina again in 1961 it is that of a revolutionary internationalist.

E rnesto and Calica crossed from northern Argentina into southern Bolivia at La Quiaca, not far from where Ernesto would some 13 years later establish a base of operations for the revolutionary guerrilla movement he hoped would liberate the entire continent of South America.

From La Quiaca, Ernesto and Calica traveled by rail to La Paz. They arrived in the Bolivian capital just a year after the country had undergone a dramatic popular revolution in which the major foreign-owned mines had been nationalized and the peasants had taken possession of the feudal estates on which they had formerly labored as unpaid serfs and tenant farmers. Thus, Ernesto found La Paz fi lled with revolutionary political fervor and excitement. In his diary, he wrote:

The widest range of adventurers of all nationalities vegetate and prosper in the midst of a colorful mestiza city that is leading the country to its destiny. The "well-to-do" refi ned people are shocked at what has been happening and complain bitterly about the new importance conferred on Indians and mestizos, but in all of them I thought I could detect a spark of nationalist enthusiasm for some of what the government has done. (pages 4–5)

Soon after their arrival in La Paz, they met a group of Argentine exiles who had been forced to leave Argentina because of their opposition to the Perón regime. One of these exiles was a young lawyer named Ricardo Rojo. They meet again in Lima, Peru, and Ecuador and then again in

Guatemala. Years later, Rojo wrote about his friendship with Ernesto and the experiences they had together in Latin America (Rojo 1968). Rojo recalls that when he met Ernesto in La Paz, he was living in a miserable rented room in one of the oldest parts of the city. Ernesto was spending most of his time visiting ancient Incan ruins or passing the day in the noisy cafés along the capital's main boulevard, Avenida 16 de Julio. From these cafés, Ernesto, Ricardo, and Calica were able to look out on the broad and sunny boulevard and watch the continuous parade of the Bolivian people as they stopped to look at the large signs propagandizing the revolutionary goals of the new regime.

On the basis of what he saw and learned while he was there, Ernesto developed a pessimistic view of the fate of the Bolivian revolution. He regarded the new regime as merely reformist and not truly revolutionary. On one occasion, Ernesto visited the Ministry of Peasant Affairs, where he saw long lines of peasants waiting to be given an audience. They were being methodically sprayed with DDT to rid them of lice.

As he saw things, this situation refl ected the fact that the new government's leaders were not solving the root causes of Bolivia's problems. They were merely trying to ameliorate the effects of these problems and calm the country's discontented masses. Thus, in the case of the peasants, the government was spraying them to rid them of lice rather than pursuing policies that would genuinely improve the social and economic conditions that were the cause of their poverty and their lack of proper hygiene.

A t this point in his political development, Ernesto was neither a Marxist nor a revolutionary. He was defi nitely a political nonconformist with a keen sense of social justice, but these traits had not yet led him to espouse any particular political cause or ideology. Rojo recalls that, when they fi rst met, Ernesto was uncertain about what he wanted to do with his life, although he was very sure about what he did not want to do with it. According to Rojo, Ernesto demanded that his traveling companions be willing to walk interminably, be devoid of any concern for the condition of their clothing, and accept without anguish the state of being absolutely without money.

I n September 1953, Ernesto and Calica left Bolivia for Peru. They went to visit Machu Picchu, the lost city of the Incas, and Cuzco, both of which Ernesto wanted to revisit. He noted in his diary that he missed Alberto. He wrote: "Despite Calica's enthusiasm for this place, I still miss Alberto's company," and, he added, "the way in which our characters were so suited to each other is becoming more obvious to me here in Machu-Picchu" (page 13). They went to Lima, where they visited Dr. Pesce and the people at the leprosarium, who received them very cordially.

They bumped into Rojo in Lima and made plans to meet up again in Guayaquil, Ecuador. While in Lima, Ernesto wrote his leftist friend from medical school in Buenos Aires, Tita Infante, an interesting letter on September 3, 1953, in which he described his visit to Bolivia. He wrote: "Bolivia is a country that has given a major example to the American continent," and "the fi ghting still goes on, and almost every night people are wounded by gunfi re on one side or the other. But the government is supported by the armed people, so there is no possibility of liquidating an armed movement from outside; it can succumb only as a result of internal dissensions" (page 17).

A s Richard Gott notes: "Guevara was intrigued by what he saw [in

Bolivia], but he was far from impressed by the caliber of Bolivia's revolutionary leadership" and "he guessed rightly that this was not a revolution that would challenge the hegemony of the United States in Latin America" (page xvi). Gott also points out that in Ernesto's letter to Tita Infante (who had been a member of the Young Communists in their medical school in Buenos Aires) Ernesto reveals that his interest in the possibility of revolutionary change has been sparked by the revolution in Bolivia, but on the other hand he is also disappointed by what he has seen and is aware of the signs of corruption and internal confl icts within the leadership of the Bolivian government (page xvii).

W hen they arrived in Ecuador's port city of Guayaquil, Ernesto and Calica met up with Rojo, who was accompanied by three leftist Argentine law students. Rojo took Ernesto and Calica to the boardinghouse where they were staying, and according to Ernesto's diary the six of them formed a "student circle" and drank their last supply of maté. Rojo and his friends showed enthusiasm for the revolutionary government in Guatemala, which they said was more radical than anything they had witnessed in Bolivia. One of these students, Eduardo "Gualo" García, jokingly suggested that Ernesto and Calica should go with him to Guatemala to see for themselves what kind of revolution was taking place there.

Ernesto wrote in his diary: "The idea [of going to Guatemala] was lying there somewhere, it only needed that little push for me to make up my mind." Initially, Calica was planning to go with Ernesto to Guatemala by way of Panama, but after they started having problems obtaining visas for traveling by ship from Guayaquil to Panama, Calica took off for Quito, the capital of Ecuador, to wait for

Ernesto there. Meanwhile, Ernesto, Gualo García, and one of the other Argentine students stayed in Guayaquil trying to arrange passage on a ship bound for Panama and obtain their visas from the Panamanian consulate. After much diffi culty, they succeeded, Ernesto having to sell most of the items in his luggage to pay for his passage and his visa. By this time, Rojo and the other Argentine student had already left for Panama by air and Calica had left Quito for Colombia.

E rnesto and Gualo didn't reach Guatemala until the end of December 1953, having spent a number of weeks on the way there in Panama and Costa Rica, where Ernesto met Juan Bosch, the famous revolutionary nationalist leader of the Dominican Republic; the exiled Venezuelan political leader Rómulo Betancourt; and the Costa Rican Communist leader Manuel Mora Valverde. Along the way, they hitchhiked, took trains, walked, and bummed passage on a boat nicknamed the *Pachuca* (because it transported *pachucos,* or down-and-outs). When they stopped in the Costa Rican port of Golfi to, which at the time belonged to the American-owned United Fruit Company, Ernesto noted in his diary: "The town is divided into clearly defi ned zones, with guards who can prevent anyone from moving across, and of course the best zone is for the gringos" (page 29). He also noted that in the hospital "the degree of comfort depends on the grade of the person working in the company" and "as always, the class spirit of the gringos makes itself felt."

A fter his discussion of Costa Rican politics with the Communist leader Mora Valverde, he wrote the following comments in his diary about the infl uence of the United Fruit Company and the U.S. government on the country's politics:

Calderón Guardia [the former president of Costa Rica] is a rich man who came to power with the support of United Fruit and local landowners. He ruled for two years until the Second World War, when Cost Rica sided with the Allied powers. The fi rst measure taken by the [U.S.] State Department was to demand the confi scation of lands in the hands of German owners, especially if coffee was grown on it. This was done, and the subsequent selling of the land led to obscure deals involving some of Calderón Guardia's ministers—deals which lost him the support of the country's landowners, but not of United Fruit. Those who work for the company are anti-Yankee, as a reaction against its exploitation. (page 31)

He also noted that the Costa Rican chief of police was "a Cuban colonel and FBI [Federal Bureau of Investigation] agent imposed by the United States."

W ith reference to José Figueres Ferrer, the three-time Costa Rican president, who was educated in the United States and backed by the U.S. government, Ernesto wrote: "In Mora's view, Figueres has a number of good ideas, but because they lack any scientifi c basis he keeps going astray. He divides the United States into two: the State Department (very just) and the capitalist trusts (the dangerous octopuses). Ernesto added a series of questions: 'What will happen when Figueres sees the light and stops having any illusions about the goodness of the United States? Will he fi ght or give up? This is the dilemma. We shall see' " (page 34).

A s Ernesto and Gualo were hitchhiking in Costa Rica, a car with Boston University license plate holders stopped to pick them up. In the car were Rojo and two friends from Argentina who were on their way to Guatemala, where they planned to sell the car. After several minor incidents crossing borders, lots of tire punctures, diffi culties from lack of money, and sleeping outdoors, they fi nally arrived in Guatemala City. They found lodgings in a boardinghouse where they didn't have to pay in advance since they had run out of money. They celebrated Christmas Eve at the house of a Guatemalan agronomist married to an Argentine woman, and Ernesto spent the next week suffering from an asthma attack that lasted until New Year's Eve.

Rojo introduced Ernesto and Gualo García to a Peruvian exile, Hilda Gadea (Ernesto's future wife), and asked her if she could help the two fi nd a place to stay. Hilda had received political asylum in Guatemala and was working as an economist for the Guatemalan government. She was a militant member of Peru's leftist political party APRA (American Popular Revolutionary Alliance), and she had been forced to fl ee Peru because the dictatorial regime of General Manuel Odría had outlawed her party and persecuted its members. She was one of a group of Peruvians who had been offered political asylum and employment by the Guatemalan government. At this point, Guatemala was a refuge for leftist political exiles from all over Latin America.

Hilda's description of their fi rst meeting is as follows:

Guevara and [Gualo] García were both in their mid-twenties, thin, and taller than the average Latin American. Guevara had dark brown hair, framing a pale face and fair features that emphasized his striking black eyes. Both were good-natured and easy-going, and Guevara had a commanding voice but a fragile appearance. His movements were quick and agile, but he gave the impression of always being relaxed. I noticed his intelligent and penetrating look and the preciseness of his comments. (Gadea 2008:24)

Hilda also noted they were dressed in casual clothes and looked more like students than professional men, but as she talked with them she realized they were well educated. Nevertheless, her fi rst impression of Ernesto was on balance negative since he seemed to her to be "superfi cial, egotistical and conceited." A few days later, she learned that his behavior when they fi rst met was infl uenced by the fact that he did not like asking favors and he was suffering from an asthma attack. This information changed her opinion of him, and she "felt a special concern for him because of his condition."

Through Hilda and her friends in Guatemala City, Ernesto was introduced to a large circle of politically and intellectually interesting people. Some of them were Guatemalans who were government offi cials or political activists and some were members of the different Latin American political exile groups who were then living in Guatemala. Hilda and Ernesto soon became close friends and confi dants. He told her about his original plan to join his friend Alberto Granado in Caracas but said that he had changed his mind about joining Alberto after he visited Bolivia because he wanted to learn more about revolutionary political conditions in Latin America, particularly the radical reforms being undertaken by the current government in Guatemala. (It is important to note here that his trip to Bolivia in 1953 changed his destiny and set him on a path that would ultimately return him to this country 13 years later to meet his death there in 1967.)

H e also told Hilda about his childhood friends and his girlfriend Chichina Ferreyra in Córdoba, whom he said he had loved but could never marry because he could not live a bourgeois life in a provincial city of Argentina. He told Hilda about his family, and she was impressed by the fact that when he spoke of his family it was always with great warmth and affection. She noted "his tie with his mother was very deep." He told her in humorous terms that "the old lady liked to go around with a bunch of intellectual women" and "they may turn out to be lesbians," but she said he always spoke with "a tone of admiration and deep affection for the old lady," a term that he explained the Argentines commonly used for their mothers. Ernesto's love for his family, she said, made her appreciate his humanity since he was always "generous and tender" toward them despite the frequent cynicism and irony he used to describe them and himself (Gadea 2008:41). He also impressed her with his ideas about the proper role of doctors in Latin America, who he felt "should not be pampered professionals, taking care of only the privileged classes," but should instead dedicate their knowledge and skills to ending the malnutrition and the illnesses associated with the extreme poverty and fi lth in which the majority of the population of the region lived.

Among the various political exiles Ernesto met through Hilda were a group of Cubans who had been involved in the unsuccessful assault led by Fidel Castro on the Moncada military barracks in Santiago de Cuba on July 26, 1953. Both Hilda and Ernesto respected the Cuban exiles for their honest simplicity and the strength of their convictions. They were especially impressed by Antonio "Ñico" López. As Hilda later wrote, these Cubans "had hardly any political indoctrination—almost all of them were workers—yet they boasted the short but outstanding accomplishment of the Moncada attack." She said Ñico stood out not only on account of his tall and slender fi gure but also because of his deep conviction that "one had to make a revolution, and that in Cuba this revolution was going to be made by Fidel"

(Gadea 2008:30). In fact, he told her: "Fidel is the greatest and most honest man born in Cuba since Martí [José Martí, famous leader of Cuba's struggle for independence from Spain]. He will make the revolution." As Hilda noted, political history subsequently proved Ñico right.

T hat Ñico and his comrades had taken part in the well-known attack on the Moncada army barracks gave them a special respected position among the other exiles, and they won Ernesto's admiration too. In his diary, Ernesto wrote that he felt small when he heard the Cubans making "grand assertions with total calmness" about making a revolution in their country. And after going to a political meeting with them where they had each taken turns speaking at the microphone, he wrote: "I can make a speech ten times more objective and without banalities: I can do it better and I can convince the public that I am saying something true. But I don't convince myself, whereas the Cubans do. Ñico left his heart and soul in the microphone and for that reason fi red even a skeptic like myself with enthusiasm" (Guevara 2001:45).

Also in Hilda's circle of friends and acquaintances was a North American professor named Harold White. He had written a book on Marxism and was looking for someone who could help him translate it into Spanish. White asked Hilda to help him, but because she knew Ernesto needed some money to pay his bills, she convinced White to hire him. In reality, they translated the book together since she knew more English than Ernesto and he knew more about Marxism than she did (Gadea 2008:53–54).

Ernesto wrote in his dairy that through Hilda he had met a "strange gringo [North American] who writes stuff about Marxism and has it translated into Spanish" (Guevara 2001:38). He noted that he had made $25 helping him and that he was "giving English-Spanish lessons to the gringo." As the days passed, the three of them became close friends, and Hilda later wrote that White had a great deal of infl uence on Ernesto's thinking during this period. In her book about their life together, she wrote: "The three of us began going on Sunday picnics, during which time it became the custom to have long discussions between Ernesto, with his crude English, and White on subjects that ranged from the international situation to Marxism, Lenin, Engels, Stalin, Freud, science in the Soviet Union, and Pavlov's conditioned refl exes" (Gadea 2008:54). As their friendship developed, Ernesto told her: "This is a good gringo. He is tired of capitalism and wants to lead a new life." By this time he had developed a strong dislike for most of the gringos he had encountered and the United States' role in Latin America and the world, but Ernesto's friendship with White reveals that he was not prejudiced against all North Americans. In fact, several years later, after Che had become an important member of the new revolutionary government in Cuba, he invited White to come to Cuba, and White lived there until his death in 1968 (Guevara 2001:38).

I n fact, according to Hilda their friendship with White "developed so well that at one point he, with his North American practicality, suggested that we should rent a house where the three of us could live, and very generously offered to pay the rent." Hilda said: "Ernesto was also enthusiastic about the idea [since] this would solve his lodging problem." However, Hilda didn't "share their enthusiasm because it would mean taking care of a house," and since she was working and involved in political activities she wanted to use her spare time to study rather than do housekeeping. In an effort to convince her to accept White's offer, Ernesto promised Hilda he would not make any advances toward her if the three of them lived together in the same house. At this point they were not yet lovers. Ernesto had hinted he was romantically interested in her, but she had not encouraged him.

I n the book she wrote about her life with Ernesto, Hilda recounts a particular outing when they went with White to a picturesque town that was a considerable distance from Guatemala City. When they were ready to return to the city they found that because a religious celebration was being held in the town all the buses going back to the city were fi lled. White suggested they should stay overnight in a local hotel until the next day, but Hilda protested and Ernesto promised he would fi nd some way for her to return to the city, which he did. She said this gesture heightened her opinion of him and made her remember he had warned her at the beginning of their friendship about how men often lie to women. He had noticed that one of her Peruvian friends was constantly fl irting with her, so he took her aside and told her: "Be careful, he is married; you know men always lie" (Gadea 2008:55).

At the end of February 1954, Ricardo Rojo and Gualo García decided to leave Guatemala, but Ernesto chose to remain in Guatemala City because of his interest in Hilda and the revolutionary programs of the Guatemalan regime. During this period, Ernesto had almost no money and great diffi culty paying for food and lodging since he couldn't fi nd a job and had no income. He tried to obtain employment as a doctor in one of the government's public health programs. In particular, he was interested in working with a program that was being carried out among the indigenous (Indian) population in the remote El Petén region of Guatemala. One of the reasons he was interested in working in this area was his desire to explore the ancient Mayan ruins there. However, he was frustrated by the Ministry of Health not validating his medical credentials unless he took another year of medical studies in Guatemala. He also had diffi culty getting a job because he was not offi cially a political exile, did not have a residence visa, had no affi liation with any of the political parties and organizations that were allied with the Guatemalan government, and was frequently confi ned to bed for days at a time because of his debilitating asthma attacks.

A t one point, Hilda remembers he was offered a position in the government's department of statistics as a result of her introducing him to one of her friends, Herbert Zeissig, who was an infl uential member of the Guatemalan Communist Party, which had a number of members working in the department. She recalls that everything went fi ne until she informed Ernesto that Zeissig had told her that he would have to join the party if he wanted the job (Anderson:138). According to Hilda, Ernesto responded angrily that she should tell Zeissig "when I want to join the party I will do so on my own initiative, not out of any ulterior motive." She admired his reaction because even though he needed the job to survive he was incapable of doing anything that was contrary to his moral principles even if it hurt his own personal interests. He did not get the job, and he later told her: "It's not that I disagree with the Communist ideology, it's the method I don't like. They shouldn't get members this way. It's all false" (Gadea:62–63).

I n mid-March 1954, Ernesto asked Hilda to be his girlfriend and suggested that later on they might get married. He said that if it was up to him, he would like to get married immediately. He gave her a handwritten poem that was a formal proposal of marriage. Hilda told him that she "also loved him, but not enough to marry him just yet," since the most important thing for her at that time was the political struggle in Guatemala and in her own country. In her book about her life with Che, she wrote: "The decision of marriage was a very diffi cult one for me; fi rst, I had to accomplish something for society, and to do that I had to be free. He answered that those were *Aprista* [member of the APRA party] prejudices, and that it was wrong to think that political activists shouldn't marry, when in effect it was a path of greater fulfi llment. He referred to Marx and Lenin, saying that marriage had not impeded them in their struggle. On the contrary, their wives supported them" (Gadea 2008:65–66). According to Hilda, Ernesto's poem was "beautiful and forceful." In it he told her "he did not desire beauty alone but, more than that, a comrade." While she did not accept his proposal for marriage at this point, they did become lovers.

A. aving failed to secure regular employment, apart from the occasional translating he did for arold White, near the end of March Ernesto joined Ñico and the other Cubans selling small items door-to-door in the provinces. He also moved into the boardinghouse that the government had established for the Cuban exiles, but within a short time Ñico and most of the Cuban exiles left for Mexico City. Since he no longer could stay in the boardinghouse, Hilda arranged for him to stay in the house of their mutual friend Helena de Holst, a political exile from Honduras who was married to a German businessman. She had a great deal of knowledge about Marxism, had visited both the Soviet Union and China, and treated Ernesto almost like a son. Helena offered to let him stay in her home without any compensation, but he gracefully refused the offer. Instead, he took his sleeping bag and started sleeping on the grounds of a nearby country club. Every morning he would come to the boardinghouse where Hilda lived to ask for hot water to make his maté. The landlady and Hilda always kept fresh fruit for him to eat, since he would not accept anything else. In the evenings he would usually return and eat only fruit or a salad, which was the strict diet he followed to avoid asthma attacks. About this time, he was offered employment as an intern in a teacher-training center run by the Ministry of Education, but he had to leave the country to renew his visa so that he could work legally in Guatemala (Gadea:67–70).

A. n a letter he wrote to his mother in April 1954 (Guevara 2001:61), he told her about his trip to neighboring El Salvador to obtain the visa that he needed to work in Guatemala. He wrote: " went with a rucksack and a briefcase, half walking, half hitching, half (shame!) paying for shelter out of the $10 that the [Guatemalan] government itself had given me. I reached El Salvador and the police confi scated some books I had bought in Guatemala, but I got through, obtained a visa (the right one this time) to enter Guatemala again, and went off to see the ruins left behind by some Mexicans, a branch of Tlascaltecas, who once came south to conquer from their center in Mexico." He noted that these ruins "are in no way comparable to the Mayan structures, still less the Incan." He also said he tried to visit Honduras, but he wrote:

The Hondurans refused me a visa just because I had residence in Guatemala, although I hardly need to tell you of my good intention to see something of a strike that has broken out there [in Honduras] and is supported by 25 percent of the whole working population (a high fi gure anywhere, but especially in a country where there is no right to strike and only underground trade unions). The fruit company [United Fruit Company] is in a fury, and of course [U.S. secretary of state John Foster] Dulles and the CIA [Central Intelligence Agency] want to intervene in Guatemala because of its terrible crime in buying weapons from wherever it wishes (the United States has not sold it a single cartridge for some time now).

Here we see the fi rst mention in his writing of the confrontation that was brewing between the governments of the United States and Guatemala.

Finally, near the end of this letter to his mother he mentioned his relationship with Hilda. He wrote: "I drink maté when there is any, and I engage in endless discussions with the comrade Hilda Gadea, an *Aprista,* whom I try to persuade in my gentle way to leave that dump of a party. She has a heart of platinum, at least. Her help is felt in everything to do with my daily life" (page 61).

I n a letter to his mother a month later, in May 1954, he wrote something quite revealing about his thoughts at the time. He said: "I could become very rich in Guatemala, but by the low method of ratifying my title [medical degree], opening a clinic and specializing in allergies (it's full of telltale colleagues here). To do that would be the most horrible betrayal of the two I's struggling inside me: the socialist and the traveler" (page 61). Here we see that he has no ambition to become a well-off physician and is increasingly developing an identity as a socialist, but he has not given up his desire to spend his foreseeable future as an adventurous traveler.

H owever, in June, the turn of events in Guatemala changed everything in his life and his plans. In his diary he wrote:

A few days ago, some aircraft from Honduras crossed the border with Guatemala and fl ew over the city in broad daylight, machine-gunning people and military objectives. I enlisted in the health brigades to help on the medical side and in the youth brigades that patrol the streets by night. The course of events was [as] follows. After the aircraft had passed, troops under the command of Colonel Castillo Armas, a Guatemalan émigré in Honduras, crossed the frontier at several points and advanced on the town of Chiquimula. . . . The invaders thought that if they just gave a shout, the whole people would come out and follow them—and for this purpose they parachuted in weapons. But in fact the people immediately rallied under the command of Arbenz [the president]. The invading troops were checked and defeated on all fronts and driven back past Chiquimula, near the Honduran frontier. [But] pirate aircraft fl ying from bases in Honduras and Nicaragua continued to machine-gun the fronts and towns. (pages 62–63)

I n the letter he wrote his mother on June 20, 1954, he gave her a similar account of these events and again wrote something about his own reaction to these events. He said: "The incident served to unite all Guatemalans behind the government and all those who, like myself, came here attracted by the country." He explained the situation as follows:

T he danger does not come from the small number of troops that have entered the country so far, nor from the warplanes that have bombed civilian homes and machine-gunned a number of people; the danger lies in how the gringos (the Yankees) are manipulating their stooges in the United Nations, since even a vague declaration would be of great help to the attackers. The Yankees have fully dropped the good-guy mask that [President Franklin D.] Roosevelt gave them and are now committing outrages in these parts. If things reach the point where it is necessary to fi ght planes and modern troops sent by the fruit company or the USA, than that is what will be done. The people's spirits are very high, and the shameless attacks, together with the lies of the international press, have united behind the government all those who used to be politically indifferent. (page 63)

Then almost insignifi cantly he added: "I myself have been assigned to emergency medical service and have also enrolled in the youth brigades to receive military instruction for any eventuality."

However, only a few days later Ernesto wrote in his diary: "A terrible cold shower has fallen on all those who admire Guatemala. On the night of Sunday, 27 June, President Árbenz announced that he was resigning. He publicly denounced the fruit company and the United States as being directly behind all the bombing and strafi ng of the civilian population." Ernesto added: "Arbenz resigned under pressure from a North American military mission that was threatening massive bombing and a declaration of war by Honduras and Nicaragua provoking United States intervention." And with regard to how this turn of events had affected him, he wrote that he expected to be expelled the next day from the small hospital where he had been working, and that "repression is coming." He also noted that "Hilda has changed her address. . . . The top people in the Guatemalan [Communist] party are seeking asylum [and] Castillo will enter the city tomorrow."

H ow did this turn of events come to pass? Before 1944, Guatemala had been just another banana republic ruled by a series of dictators who served the interests of the local landed oligarchy and the United Fruit Company—the American-owned banana company that controlled vast landholdings, railways, and ports in Central America, the Caribbean, Colombia, and Ecuador (Schlesinger and Kinzer 1982). But in 1944 the ruling strongman, the dictator Jorge Ubico, was overthrown by a popular revolt led by junior army offi cers and students. On the surface, the revolt appeared to be aimed primarily at discarding Ubico's oppressive regime in favor of more democratic rule. But in reality, the groups who participated in the revolt demanded the complete reform of Guatemala's exploitative and highly unequal economic and social order.

F ollowing the overthrow of the Ubico regime, elections were held and Juan José Arévalo became Guatemala's fi rst popularly elected president. Under Arévalo's rule a major effort was made to bring Guatemala's majority Indian population into the 20th century and a large number of rural and urban workers were unionized. The revolutionary policies of Arévalo's government were continued and in fact accelerated by his successor, Colonel Jacobo Arbenz, who was democratically elected to the presidency in 1951. By the time Ernesto arrived in Guatemala, in late 1953, the Arbenz regime had distributed thousands of hectares of uncultivated land to over 100,000 landless peasants. This land was expropriated by the government from the country's large landed estates, and included 11,000 hectares of uncultivated land that belonged to the powerful United Fruit Company, which even distributed mail in

Guatemala.

The response from the U.S. government was almost immediate. The U.S. secretary of state at the time, John Foster Dulles, had close ties to the United Fruit Company, since his law fi rm had represented the company. Moreover, his brother Allen Dulles was the director of the CIA, and John Moors Cabot, who was in charge of Inter-American Affairs in the State Department, had a brother who was the former president of the United Fruit Company.

A t the March 1954 foreign ministers' meeting of the Organization of American States (OAS), U.S. Secretary of State Dulles accused the Arbenz regime of being "Communist-infi ltrated" and claimed Arbenz intended to align Guatemala with the Soviet bloc (Schlesinger and Kinzer 1982). He succeeded in having the OAS pass the famous Resolution 93, which expressed the right of the OAS members "to take the necessary measures to protect themselves against Communist intervention" in the hemisphere. As far as the U.S. government was concerned, the "necessary measures" in the case of Guatemala involved the clandestine preparation by the CIA of a mercenary force to invade Guatemala and overthrow the democratically elected government of President Arbenz. This force was assembled in the neighboring countries of Honduras and El Salvador and received the support of the dictatorial regimes in these two countries as well as the Somoza dictatorship in nearby Nicaragua— all three of these regimes were closely tied to Washington. The CIA supplied the invaders with arms and planes and also arranged for the betrayal of the higher echelons of the Guatemalan army.

O n June 17, 1954, this force under the command of ex-army offi cer Carlos Castillo Armas crossed into Guatemala with the intent of marching on the capital. After an initial period in which the Arbenz government put up rather successful resistance, the U.S. ambassador and the high command of the army pressured Arbenz into resigning and turning over the government to several generals in the army high command. They in turn allowed Castillo Armas and his force to enter the capital unopposed. As a result, the democratically elected regime collapsed and Castillo Armas was fl own into Guatemala from Honduras on the personal plane of U.S. Ambassador John Peurifoy. The new government led by Castillo Armas was backed by the Eisenhower administration, which gave it over $80 million over the next three years. It immediately suspended Guatemala's democratic constitution and instituted a campaign of political repression directed at all the individuals and groups that had supported the Arbenz government and its reforms. The police and a "liberation force" began rounding up, imprisoning, and executing many of the former government's offi cials and supporters as well as the political exiles from other Latin American countries that were in the country. The new government also issued a decree that returned the expropriated land given to the peasants to the large landowners and the United Fruit Company.

O nce the invasion had begun, Ernesto and his friends watched in exasperation as President Arbenz naively relied on the army to repulse the invasion. He wrote the following about this situation in a letter to his mother on July 4, 1954: "Treason continues to be the birthright of the army, and once more the aphorism is confi rmed that sees the liquidation of the army as the true principle of democracy." He also wrote: "The harsh truth is that Arbenz did not know how to rise to the occasion" and "we were completely defenseless, since there were no planes, no anti-aircraft guns and no shelters." As a result, Ernesto said: "Panic gripped the people, especially 'the brave and loyal army of Guatemala' [and] Arbenz did not think to himself that a people in arms is an invincible power." He concluded with the comment: "He could have given arms to the people but he did not want to—and now we see the result" (page 67).

In the repressive aftermath of the overthrow of the Arbenz government in Guatemala, Ernesto would almost certainly have been imprisoned, and perhaps executed, if he had not taken refuge in the Argentine embassy. All the Latin American embassies were immediately fi lled with asylum seekers, especially the Argentine and Mexican embassies. Ernesto asked for and was given asylum in the Argentine embassy, where he met a number of Guatemalan offi cials and Latin American political exiles who had also received asylum and were staying in the embassy. He told Hilda he wanted to go to Mexico and afterward to China and tried to convince her that she should go with him. He said they could get married in Mexico, but she said she wanted to return home to Peru or go to Argentina and asked him for his family's address there. According to Hilda: "Ernesto insisted, laughing, that we would one day meet again in Mexico and marry" (Gadea 2008:84).

D uring the fi rst days that he was in the embassy they saw each other daily, but then one day he discovered she and the landlady at her boardinghouse had been arrested by the police. He also learned that the fi rst question the police asked Hilda was whether she knew where he was. She said they should ask at the Argentine embassy and refused to give them a description of him or identify him in the photographs they had found among her things in the boardinghouse. The police confi scated her belongings and took her to the women's prison and placed her in a cell with common criminals (pages 85–88).

W hen Ernesto found out, he wanted to surrender himself in return for her release, but the chargé d'affaires of the Argentine embassy and all of the exiles there convinced him the police would merely put him in prison too and it would do her no good. Meanwhile, Hilda went on a hunger strike, claiming she had been given political asylum in Guatemala and the authorities had brought no charges against her. Because her hunger strike was picked up by the press and several Latin American ambassadors (but not the Peruvian ambassador) visited her in jail to make sure she was being treated properly, she was released but ordered to appear before the new attorney general. He accused her of being a Communist, which she vehemently denied, and then released her on condition she appear personally before President Castillo Armas. When she went to meet him he apologized for her imprisonment and agreed to give her a safe conduct so that she could leave the country without any further diffi culties (pages 90–91).

While he was in the Argentine embassy, Ernesto received money and clothes from his family, but he refused to leave for Argentina on the planes that had been sent by the Argentine government to pick up people who had taken refuge in the embassy. Instead he asked the ambassador to obtain a safe-conduct pass for him so that he could leave the country and go to Mexico. While he was waiting for his safe-conduct pass and visa, he left the embassy to fi nd Hilda. She was having diffi culty leaving the country because the Peruvian embassy would not give her a valid passport.

T hey had a long discussion about what had happened and where they stood. Hilda wrote in her book: "On reviewing the events of that period it seemed to us that in trying to defend the goals of the Guatemalan people we had become closer than ever." She also wrote: "Our analysis of what we had experienced in Guatemala led us to the conclusion that the revolution there had failed because popular support was not sought to defend it," and "we also concluded that the right way for a revolution to maintain national sovereignty, free of the infl uence of imperialism, would be for it to arm the people to defend their gains" (page 97).

T hey also spoke about their plans, and Ernesto told Hilda: "I have not insisted lately . . . because things being the way they are, there is no possibility of starting a new life. But in Mexico we will get married. Have no doubt about it." Happily surprised by the strength of his conviction, she answered: "Do you really think so? I'm going south" (page 94). A few days later, Hilda saw Ernesto off on the train to Mexico. When she returned to the house where she had been staying, she was arrested again by the police. Much to her surprise, they told her that she was being deporting to Mexico! Unfortunately, her deportation from Guatemala was a harrowing experience, as opposed to Ernesto's relatively uneventful departure. She was taken under guard to the border and held prisoner there until she paid her captors to smuggle her across the river into Mexico (page 123).

W hen Ernesto arrived in Mexico City in mid-September 1954 he discovered that, like Guatemala during the Arbenz presidency, Mexico was a refuge for political exiles from all over Latin America. In addition to the latest infl ux of Guatemalan exiles, there were political refugees from the Dominican Republic, Cuba, Colombia, Peru, Venezuela, Haiti, and his own Argentina. Most of these exiles lived in the same neighborhoods of the city and frequented the same bars and cafés.

Since Hilda was granted political asylum by the Mexican authorities after she escaped from Guatemala, her status in the country allowed her to fi nd employment without any diffi culty. Ernesto, on the other hand, had entered the country on merely a visitor's visa and had the same diffi culties fi nding employment as in Guatemala.

Ernesto initially made ends meet as a street photographer. He became a regular member of the exile community. Through mutual contacts in Mexico City, Ernesto and Hilda were reunited in late October shortly after she arrived in the city. Hilda's account of their meeting reveals they did not get off to a good start: "Again Ernesto spoke of the possibility of getting married. I said we should wait. I had just arrived in Mexico and wanted to adjust to the new environment and look for a job. I really was not yet certain. I think he realized this and seemed somewhat bothered by it. I had the feeling that my ambiguous answer had created a certain tension, because he then said we would just be friends. I was a little surprised: I was only asking him to wait. But I accepted his decision. I had just arrived, and here we were, already quarreling" (page 125).

H. owever, over the next few months they did see each other frequently and they discussed their Guatemalan experiences often. They both had developed a deep sense of disdain for the U.S. government, which they blamed for the overthrow of the Arbenz regime, the political repression that followed in Guatemala, and most of Latin America's economic and political ills. Ernesto told ilda he had obtained a position as an assistant in the allergy ward of the general hospital in Mexico City, which paid very little but allowed him to practice medicine. He also told her he was in touch with Ñico López, who had by chance come into the allergy ward at the hospital one day with another Cuban. He said they embraced each other as old friends reunited. Ñico told him that he and his Cuban friends in Mexico were in constant contact with the revolutionary 26th of July Movement in Cuba, and they expected Fidel Castro and his brother Raúl would soon be released from prison there and might come to Mexico.

A. n a letter he wrote his mother in November 1954, it is possible to get a sense of what Ernesto was thinking at this period in his life. He told her he enjoyed being in Mexico but still hoped to go to Europe. He also said that while he had not "lost a bit of contempt for the United States" he wanted "to get to know New York at least," but then added he felt sure he would "leave just as anti-Yankee" as when he arrived there (Guevara 2001:87). At the end of the letter he also said that "in the hecatomb that Guatemala became after the fall [of President Arbenz]— where everyone expected to fend only for himself—the Communists kept their faith and comradeship alive and are the only group still working there." And then he said: " think they deserve respect and sooner or later I will join the Party myself. What most prevents me from doing it right now is that I have a huge desire to travel in Europe, and I would not be able to do that if I was subject to rigid discipline [as a member of the party]."

Ernesto and Hilda grew closer and toward the end of December became lovers again. As a New Year's present, he gave her a copy of the Argentine writer José Hernández's epic poem about a gaucho called "Martin Fierro," which he had frequently recited and applied to the reality of their own lives since they fi rst met. In the fl yleaf he wrote the following inscription: "To Hilda, so that on the day we part the substance of my hopes for the future and my predestined struggle will remain with you" (Gadea 2008:134). She tried to hide her emotion, but confessed she was deeply moved by this inscription.

H e continued to insist they should get married. She resisted at fi rst, but within a few months realized she really did want to marry him, so they made plans to marry in May 1955. However, they had diffi culty obtaining permission from the Mexican government since they were not Mexican citizens and had different nationalities. They decided to live together until they could get married offi cially. They rented a small fl at in a section of the city where most of the Latin American political exiles were living. One night, Ernesto brought Raúl Castro home with him. Ñico had introduced them shortly after Raúl arrived in Mexico. Hilda's account of this meeting provides an invaluable description of him: "Despite his youth—he was twenty-three or twenty-four years old at the time—and even younger appearance, blond and beardless and looking like a university student, his ideas were very clear as to how the revolution was to be made and, more important, for what purpose and for whom. He had great faith in Fidel, not because he was his brother but because of his political leadership. It was his faith in Fidel that had led him to participate in the Moncada attack" (page 143).

He told Hilda that he was convinced that an armed struggle was necessary since one could not expect to take power through elections in Cuba and most of Latin America. However, he said this armed struggle would have to be carried out in close association with the populace, since it would only succeed with the support of the people. Once power had been taken with the support of the people, he said it would then be possible to transform Cuba's capitalist society into a socialist society. According to Hilda, Raúl had Communist ideas and was an admirer of the Soviet Union. She said: "He fi rmly believed that the power struggle must benefi t the people" and this struggle would have to be against U.S.

imperialism, not only for Cuba but in all of Latin America (page 143).

T hereafter, Hilda noticed that Ernesto saw Raúl almost every day, and they learned Fidel was coming to Mexico. Raúl told them about how they had begun to organize the 26th of July Movement. She said "it was spirit lifting just to talk to him," since he was always "joyful, communicative, sure of himself, and very clear in his ideas." For this reason, she said, he and Ernesto got along very well. Early in July, Fidel arrived in Mexico, and Ernesto met him at the home of a Cuban woman married to a Mexican. They ended up talking for almost 10 hours straight through the night, exchanging ideas about Latin American and international affairs. According to Hilda, Ernesto said Fidel had a deep faith in Latin America and that he was a new type of political leader who was modest, knew where he wanted to go, and had great tenacity and fi rmness. She said Ernesto discovered that he was a "true Latin American" and "he also found in Fidel a deep conviction that in fi ghting against [the Cuban dictator Fulgencio] Batista, he was fi ghting the imperialist monster that kept Batista in power" (page 144). In the journal he was keeping at the time, Ernesto wrote: "I met Fidel Castro, the Cuban revolutionary. He is a young, intelligent guy, very sure of himself and extraordinarily audacious; I think we hit it off well" (Guevara 2001:99).

L ater, Ernesto told Hilda: "Ñico was right in Guatemala when he told us that if Cuba had produced anything good since Martí it was Fidel Castro. He will make the revolution. We are in complete agreement. . . . I could only fully support someone like him." She said that after the fi rst day they met, Ernesto and Fidel began meeting together three or four times a week, but they had to be secretive because the Cuban exiles in Mexico were being watched and might be jailed since it was not only Batista's police but also the FBI who were watching them. Hilda met Fidel for the fi rst time when he came to a dinner party that she and Ernesto arranged for him. Again, her account of this meeting provides an invaluable description of this important fi gure at an early stage in his political career: "He was young, only thirty, fair-skinned, and tall, about six foot two, and solidly built. . . . He did not look like the leader one knew him to be. He could very well have been a handsome bourgeois tourist. When he talked, however, his eyes shone with passion and revolutionary zeal, and one could see why he could command the attention of listeners. He had the charm and personality of a great leader, and at the same time an admirable simplicity and naturalness. . . . We were all in awe of him, except Ernesto, who had already spoken with him at length" (page 145).

H. ilda asked Fidel why he had come to Mexico. e told her that he had come there to organize and train a group of fi ghters that would invade Cuba and confront Batista's army, which was backed by the Yankees. He said that his invading group of fi ghters would call on the Cuban people to help them overthrow the corrupt Batista dictatorship and that they were organizing clandestine support committees in the country as well as overseas to help them. At the end of his explanation he told her: "The struggle in Cuba was part of the continental fi ght against the Yankees, a fi ght that [Simón] Bolívar and Martí had foreseen." After he fi nished, Hilda said she was absolutely convinced and ready to accompany them. Afterward, she asked Ernesto if Fidel would take women in his invasion force, and he said: "Perhaps women like you—but it would be very diffi cult." A few days later, he asked her what she thought of "this crazy idea of the Cubans, invading an island completely defended by coastal artillery?" She realized that he was asking her opinion about whether he should join the expedition. Even though it would mean their separation and would be very dangerous, she said: "It is crazy, but one must go along." He embraced her and said the reason he asked her this question was because he wanted to know what she would say, since he had decided to join Fidel's force as their doctor (page 147). Hilda said that from this point on, Ernesto spoke of nothing but the Cuban Revolution and that in the end she lost her husband to this cause.

According to Fidel, Ernesto joined the 26th of July Movement the night they fi rst met in Mexico City. The following is Fidel's account of this meeting: "Because of his state of mind when he left Guatemala, because of the extremely bitter experience he'd lived through there—that cowardly aggression against the country, the interruption of a process that had awakened the hopes of the people—because of his revolutionary avocation, his spirit of struggle . . . in a matter of minutes Che decided to join [our] small group of Cubans who were working on organizing a new phase of the struggle in our country" (Deutschmann 1994:99).

I. n early August, Hilda realized that she was pregnant. When she told Ernesto, he was very happy and said that they needed to hurry up and get married and let their parents know. They made arrangements to get married at the Argentine embassy but at the last minute Ernesto asked a doctor at the hospital where he was working to marry them since he was also the mayor of the beautiful little town of Tepotzotlán outside Mexico City. On August 18, 1955, they were married in Tepotzotlán. Raúl Castro accompanied them as well as a Venezuelan poet named Lucila Velasquez, a friend of Hilda's, and Jesús Montané, a member of the 26th of July Movement who had just arrived from Cuba to serve as treasurer of the movement and aide to Fidel.

H ilda recalled years later in her book about her life with Ernesto that their marriage ceremony in Tepotzotlán was simple, intimate, and full of warm comradeship. When they all returned from the wedding, Ernesto prepared an Argentine-style roast dinner, which Fidel attended. Over the next few days, they told their friends about their wedding and sent cables to their parents in Argentina and Peru. Hilda's parents sent them some money and a letter scolding them for not having invited them to the wedding. Ernesto wrote to Hilda's parents and thanked them for their generous gift and described their future plans as follows:

"First we will wait for 'Don Ernesto.' (If it's not a boy, there's going to be trouble.) Then we'll consider a couple of fi rm propositions I have, one in Cuba, the other a fellowship in France, depending upon Hilda's ability to travel around. Our wandering life isn't over yet and before we defi nitely settle in Peru, a country that I admire in many ways, or in Argentina, we want to see a bit of Europe and two fascinating countries, India and China. I am particularly interested in New China because it refl ects my own political ideals" (Gadea 2008:153–54). In another section of this rather lengthy letter, Ernesto wrote about their relationship as equals: "Our married life probably won't be like yours. Hilda works eight hours a day and I, somewhat irregularly, around twelve. I'm in research, the toughest branch (and poorest paid). But our routines work harmoniously together and have turned our home into a free association between two equals."

F idel left Mexico for a time to seek support from Cubans living in the United States who opposed the Batista dictatorship. From these Cuban exiles he collected funds and recruits for his planned invasion, and when he returned to Mexico he obtained the services of a Colonel Alberto Bayo to train his group in the tactics of guerrilla warfare. Colonel Bayo had been born in Cuba and had served as an offi cer in the Spanish Republican Army. During the Spanish Civil War, he had gained a great deal of experience in guerrilla warfare and later he had collaborated in Latin American efforts to launch an armed popular struggle.

T oward the end of 1955, the meetings between Ernesto, Raúl, Fidel, and the other Cubans became more frequent, and they often met at the apartment where Ernesto and Hilda lived. Fidel arranged to have all his mail sent to their address under Hilda's maiden name. Consequently, Ernesto warned Hilda to be careful with the mail addressed to her, especially if it came from Cuba or the United States. On Christmas Eve 1955, they attended a dinner prepared by Fidel, who spoke at some length about the projects that would be carried out in Cuba once the revolution had succeeded. According to Hilda: "He spoke with such certainty and ease that one had the feeling we were already in Cuba, carrying out the process of construction. . . . Suddenly as if by design, there was silence. Fidel's last words still echoed in my mind. I looked at Ernesto and he returned the glance. In his eyes I could read the same thoughts that were going through my mind. In order to carry out all these plans, it was fi rst necessary to get to Cuba. . . . This meant many diffi culties, great efforts, and sacrifi ces—all the dangers that must be undergone to achieve the power for revolutionary change" (page 168).

In the silence, Hilda said it was possible to sense the thoughts of everyone in the room. They all wanted Fidel's plans to come true, but they were painfully aware of the enormous costs in pain, suffering, and death that would be necessary for these plans to be realized. For Hilda, the sacrifi ce would be, in her own words, "terribly painful" since it would mean separation from her new husband and the father of her child and waiting with "agonized awareness" of the constant dangers he would face. She also worried about the "marvelous group of comrades" whom she had grown to love and what could happen to them. But at the same time she said that she "felt proud of them and what they were about to do for the liberation of Cuba, the fi rst stage in the liberation of [the] continent" (page 168).

I n January 1956, they began almost daily preparations for their expedition to Cuba. Ernesto started eating lightly to keep his weight down— just meat, salad, and fruit, which was his favorite diet anyway. He gave up his allergy research and turned down a lectureship in physiology so that he had more time to go with the Cubans to a gymnasium where they practiced judo, wrestling, and karate. In addition, he started reading extensively about economics. Each week he would read a book and then discuss it with Hilda, since she was an economist and knew most of the books he was reading. He also asked her to teach him to type, which she did. They discussed seriously the implications of his commitment to participate in the mission to invade Cuba. It would mean giving up their plans to go to Africa on the fellowship, which he had previously applied for from the Pan American Health Offi ce. In fact, it meant abandoning all their plans.

For Hilda, it was now completely clear that he was going to participate in the expedition to create a popular revolution in Cuba. She accepted this commitment and realized it was part of a larger commitment to "fi ght against Yankee imperialism" in all of Latin America. She saw it as only the fi rst stage of the liberation of the continent, and realized that "afterward, the struggle would have to be continued in the other countries." She was in total accord with this commitment on the part of Ernesto, even though she knew that it would not be possible for her to participate in the Cuban expedition because she had to take care of their child. She was willing to help as best she could— "by supporting the movement and carrying on propaganda activities" (page 172).

On February 15, 1956, Hilda gave birth to their child, a girl. Ernesto was with her the entire time, including in the delivery room. They had agreed that if the baby was a boy, she would choose his name, but if it was a girl, he would choose her name. He chose the name Hilda Beatriz. The fi rst name, Hilda, was in his wife's honor, and the second name was in honor of his favorite aunt, Beatriz Guevara. Fidel was their fi rst visitor in the hospital and like Ernesto he was enchanted with the baby. He held her in his arms and said: "This girl is going to be educated in Cuba," and he said it with such conviction that Hilda felt sure it would happen (page 173).

Ernesto became a doting father and rushed home every day to watch and play with her. When the baby was only a few weeks old, Hilda came down with a bad cold and a high fever. Ernesto stayed home and immediately took over the care of Hildita (little Hilda). According to Hilda, he always showed great concern for both her and Hildita and consistently gave them tender and affectionate care. During this period, they read books together about wars of liberation and the Chinese revolution, and Russian novels about the struggle against the Nazis in Russia and Eastern Europe during World War II. On the basis of their readings, they concluded that guerrilla warfare might be the best way for a popular revolution to succeed in Latin America.

With Colonel Bayo's assistance, Fidel established a secret training camp for his group at a large ranch in the mountainous Chalco district outside of Mexico City. Fidel brought 80 men to this training camp, including Ernesto. Within a short time, Colonel Bayo singled out Ernesto as his best student. It was during this training period that Ernesto's Cuban comrades gave him the nickname "Che." They called him Che because like most Argentines he used the word *che* constantly, which is similar to "Hey, buddy!" in English and is used by most Argentines at the beginning of a sentence to catch someone's attention or express familiarity. Ernesto accepted this nickname with pride.

In April 1956, after their military training the group began studying Marxist literature and discussing the problems of Cuba and Latin America. Che (Ernesto) came home only on the weekends. In late May, he told Hilda they were going somewhere for fi eld training and they might depart from there for the invasion of Cuba. About a week afterward, she saw an article in the Mexico City newspapers about the arrest of Fidel and four of his Cuban companions because their immigration papers were not in order. Hilda suspected that trouble was brewing, so she collected all their papers and books in their apartment and took them to a friend's house. Shortly thereafter, two men came to her door and asked her if she was Hilda Gadea. She answered that she was Hilda Gadea Guevara. They asked her about the mail she received and told her she had received a telegram that was compromising. They wanted her to come with them, but when she said she was nursing a four-month-old child and she would have to bring the baby with her, they told her she did not have to go with them at that moment. They said she should wait until they came back. When they left, she immediately sent word through one of the Cubans to warn the others that she was under police surveillance (Gadea 2008:185–86).

Later that evening, the same two men returned and took her and the baby to the federal police offi ce in the center of the city. There she was questioned about a telegram from Cuba that had been sent to her address. One of the interrogators was a Cuban who said he had sent the telegram. They asked her where her husband was, who were the visitors to her house, and whether she was involved in politics. She told them she was a political exile and they should notify the Mexican senator who had signed her asylum papers. She also complained they were violating her rights, asked for a lawyer, and said her daughter's health was being endangered by detaining them both in uncomfortable conditions. They took her into a dark interrogation room where she was forced to sit, with the baby in her arms, looking into a bright light. They asked her a series of questions intended to prove that her husband and the Cubans were Communists. She had the impression one of the people in the room was a CIA or an FBI agent. They fi nally let her return to her apartment after they failed to get the information they wanted from her and saw that they could not intimidate her.

T he two policemen who took her back to the apartment stayed there with her all night. The next morning they took her and the baby back to the federal police headquarters and she was again interrogated. They tried to convince her she should save herself and the baby by telling them everything they wanted to know about her husband and his Cuban friends. She refused to give them any information and asked again for a lawyer. Fidel and his four companions were in the same building, and they discovered she was being detained there too. Later in the day she was taken to the police chief's offi ce and found Fidel there. He greeted her affectionately and told her: "I can't allow you to be here with the baby. Please tell them that you receive letters for me—being a political exile, I had no permanent address and had asked you to receive mail for me, addressed to you." She hesitated, but he said: "You make this statement so that you'll be freed, because I can't let you and the baby go through these discomforts and dangers" (page 186). After he insisted, she signed the statement and they let her go.

L ater she discovered that the former president of Mexico Lázaro Cárdenas had intervened on Fidel's behalf. She also learned that Fidel had agreed to take the police to the ranch where Ernesto and the others were hiding in order to avoid a gunfi ght and bloodshed. Fidel arranged with the federal police to go in fi rst and prepare the group to surrender without a fi ght. Fortunately, when Fidel went to the ranch with the police, Raúl and half the group were not at the ranch and escaped being taken by the police. They also hid the group's weapons so that the police were not able to fi nd them.

Fidel and the group (including Che) that were captured at the ranch were all taken to the Immigration Detention Center in Mexico City, where they were interrogated and held as prisoners. When Hilda discovered where he was being held prisoner and went to visit him, he told her: "There is no doubt the FBI is mixed up in this, to defend Batista. He represents for them the control of the sugar industry and commerce [in Cuba]. The Mexicans can't be that interested in hunting down Cuban revolutionaries. Not only that, they have made their own revolution and they know what it is to take up arms. It's those Yankee *hijos de la chingada,* sons of bitches, as they say here who are behind this whole affair" (page 193).

Fidel, Che, and the rest of the group being detained by the Mexican authorities banded together and became a close-knit circle of comrades under the stressful conditions of their confi nement. In a letter he wrote to his mother dated July 15, 1956, Che had the following to say about the effect his imprisonment had on his feelings toward his Cuban comrades:

During these prison days and the period of training that preceded them, I have identifi ed totally with my comrades in the cause. I remember a phrase that once seemed to me idiotic or at least bizarre, referring to such a total identifi cation among the members of a fi ghting body that the very concept of the "I" disappeared and gave way to the concept of "we." It was a Communist morality and may, of course, appear to be a doctrinaire exaggeration, but in reality it was (and is) a beautiful thing to be able to feel that stirring of "we."

He also said the following in response to his mother's advice that he pursue a more moderate path and look out for himself: "You are profoundly mistaken in believing that great inventions or works of art arise out of moderation or 'moderate egoism'. Any great work requires passion, and the revolution requires passion and audacity in large doses— things that humanity as a whole does have." Near the end of this letter, he referred to his future plans. He said that after Cuba he planned to go somewhere else to carry on the revolutionary struggle against imperialism and that he would really be done for if he were to choose a career in which he would be "shut up in some bureaucratic offi ce or allergy clinic" (Guevara 2001:110–11).

After several weeks, the group of detainees decided to go on a hunger strike. In a few days, all of the group, including Fidel, were released— but not Ernesto and Calixto García, a Cuban, since the federal police claimed their immigration papers were not in order. Fidel gave the Mexican authorities a large sum of money to resolve their immigration problems and told Hilda they would have to wait a while before the federal police would release the two remaining detainees. Ernesto and Calixto were released after spending almost two months in detention.

During this period, Hilda visited him regularly with Hildita, and she later wrote that one of her fondest memories was of Che playing with their daughter during those visits. She wrote: "We met in a large patio where the prisoners could play football to keep in shape. There

I would spread out a blanket and put Hildita under an umbrella. Che played for long periods of time with Hildita until she fell asleep, then he would watch her, observing every gesture the baby made in her sleep. At other times he would pick her up and carry her proudly around the patio" (Gadea 2008:195). She said that it was during this time that Che took to calling Hildita "love's petal most profound."

Hildita was four months old when he was arrested but almost six months old when he was released. He went to their apartment and surprised both Hilda and Hildita. He told them he could spend only a short time at home since he had to go fi nish his training and go into hiding to do so, but he promised he would visit them as often as he could. When he did come home it was usually for just a few days and he would always spend as much time taking care of Hildita as he could. He started calling her "my little Mao," and he would recite poetry to her while he carried her around in his arms. According to Hilda, one day he looked at Hildita tenderly and said: "My dear daughter, my little Mao, you don't know what a diffi cult world you're going to have to live in. When you grow up, this whole continent, and maybe the whole world, will be fi ghting against the great enemy, Yankee imperialism. You will have to go fi ght. I may not be here anymore, but the struggle will enfl ame the continent." Hilda was overwhelmed by his words and embraced him (page 203).

T he last time Hilda saw Che before he left for Cuba, he returned for a weekend and they made plans to take a short trip to the beach resort of Acapulco. One of the Cubans came to the house early on Sunday morning and asked for Che. He said the police were on the hunt for them again and they would have to leave right away. Hilda had the feeling something serious was going on and asked him to tell her if something was going to happen. He told her they were only taking precautions and calmly gathered his things. When he kissed her good-bye she trembled without knowing why and drew closer to him. Later she remembered how hard he had tried to remain natural so as not to alarm her, but he never came back after that weekend.

In a letter he wrote his mother in November 1956, he said: "Still here in Mexico, I am answering your last letters. I can't give you much news about my life, because I am only doing a little gymnastics and reading a huge amount (especially things you can imagine). I see Hilda some weekends." He added: "I've given up trying to get my case resolved through legal channels, so my residence in Mexico will be only temporary. In any event, Hilda is going with the little girl to spend New Year with her family. She'll be there for a month, then we'll see what happens. My long-term aim is to see something of Europe, if possible live there, but that is getting more and more diffi cult. . . . I had a project for my life which involved ten years of wandering, then some years of medical studies and, if any time was left, the great adventure of physics. Now that is all over. The only clear thing is that the ten years of wandering look like being more (unless unforeseen circumstances put an end to my wandering), but it will be very different from the kind I imagined. Now, when I get to a new country, it won't be to look around and visit museums and ruins, but also (because that still interests me) to join the people's struggle" (Guevara 2001:111–12).

C he was one of the 82 members of the 26th of July Movement who left Mexico for Cuba the last week of November 1956. Fidel was able to obtain only one boat for this expedition. It was an old 60-foot cabin cruiser–type yacht named *Granma* that had a normal carrying capacity of only 20 persons. Some of the men who had trained for the expedition had to be left behind because Fidel could not fi t all of them on the boat. The 82 men who did get on the boat left from the Mexican port of Tuxpan under the cover of darkness shortly after midnight on November 25, 1956. After a series of diffi culties, bad weather, and mishaps that slowed their trip across the Gulf of Mexico, they disembarked on the southeastern shoreline of Cuba on December 2, 1956. The general location of this landing was the same as where Cuba's national hero José Martí had landed 61 years earlier during the struggle to liberate Cuba from Spanish colonial domination.

CHAPTER FIVE

EL CHE The Guerrila Warrior

When they fi nally reached the Cuban coastline near Cape Cruz, it was beginning to get light. The landing spot they had chosen was near the coastal town of Niquero in what was then called Oriente Province. Waiting for them there was Celia Sánchez, who was one of the founders of the 26th of July Movement and a key member of the clandestine network in Santiago de Cuba, the main city of Oriente Province. She was waiting for them with some vehicles, food, weapons, and about 50 men who were ready to join with Fidel Castro's group to attack and capture Niquero and then the neighboring town of Manzanillo.

A few days earlier, on November 30, 1956, the naval station and police station in Santiago de Cuba, the largest city in the region, had been attacked by the 26th of July Movement. This attack was a diversionary tactic to draw the army and police away from the area where the *Granma* expedition was supposed to land. But when the *Granma* arrived off the coast of Oriente Province on the morning of December 2, 1956, it was running out of fuel and was two days behind schedule. Fidel and his men were forced to beach the ship at a spot called Playa de los

Colorados, near the village of Las Coloradas, about 15 miles south of the designated landing spot. The exact spot where they beached the boat was a muddy mangrove swamp, and they were unable to unload most of their heavy weapons.

T he guerrillas were forced to abandon their heavy equipment and most of their supplies and make their way to land by wading through the muddy marsh. The following is Fidel Castro's account of this critical moment in the history of the Cuban revolution:

On two occasions, the skipper at the helm of the *Granma,* a former Cuban Navy commander who had joined our movement, tried to follow the correct route through the labyrinth marked by the buoys, and on two occasions he came back to the point of departure. He was trying a third time. It was impossible to keep up this exasperating search. There were only a few liters of fuel left. It was already broad daylight. The enemy was relentlessly searching by sea and by air. The boat was in grave danger of being destroyed a few kilometers off the coast, with all of the forces on board. We could see the coast nearby, and the waters were apparently shallow. The skipper was ordered to head straight for this spot, full steam ahead. The *Granma* ran into mud and stopped 60 meters from shore. The men disembarked with their weapons, and struggled through the water over soft mud that threatened to swallow them up as they were overloaded. (Castro 2001:21)

But as soon as they reached what had seemed to be the solid shore they encountered mud again.

T hey found themselves in a long, swampy coastal lagoon that stretched between their point of arrival and the solid land beyond. According to Castro: "It took almost two hours to cross that hellish swamp. Having just reached solid ground, the fi rst heavy weaponry shots were heard fi ring at the landing point, near the now solitary *Granma*. Its presence had been sighted and communicated to the enemy command, which immediately responded with a sea attack on the expedition and machine gunning from the air of the area to which the small expeditionary force of 82 men was headed" (Castro 2001:22). Fortunately, the mangrove thickets through which they were making their way protected them from being seen from the air. For several days they marched toward the neighboring Sierra Maestra (Cuba's largest mountain range) by hiding during the day and marching during the night. At fi rst they did not encounter any resistance, but on December 5, they were surprised by a large detachment of the army near a sugarcane fi eld at a place called Alegría de Pío, where they had stopped to rest. Because they had eaten and drunk very little since their departure from Mexico and were exhausted from the ordeal of their landing and several days of nighttime marching, they were completely unprepared to defend themselves and ran in all directions to try and save themselves.

The tragic outcome of this encounter with Batista's forces is described by Fidel Castro as follows: "A surprise enemy attack in a light forest where we were waiting for nightfall to continue the march to the Sierra Maestra. A terrible setback, total dispersion; a tenacious search and persecution of the scattered men; an enormous cost in the lives of combatants, the vast majority of them murdered after falling prisoner; almost all the weapons lost." Only Guevara, Fidel and Raúl Castro, and 12 others escaped and made their way to the Sierra Maestra. Guevara was wounded in the neck, but his wound was not serious since the bullet ricocheted off a cartridge case in his chest pocket. He survived, but with only the most rudimentary medical treatment because he had left his medical knapsack at Alegría de Pío.

I n one of the essays he later wrote and published in *Pasajes de la Guerra Revolucionaria* (*Episodes of the Revolutionary War*) , Guevara described his baptism of fi re at Alegría de Pío as follows: "Perhaps this was the fi rst time I was faced with the dilemma of choosing between my devotion to medicine and my duty as a revolutionary soldier. There at my feet was a knapsack full of medicine and a box of ammunition, I couldn't possibly carry both of them; they were too heavy. I picked up the box of ammunition, leaving the medicine, and started to cross the clearing, heading toward the cane fi eld. I remember Faustino Pérez, kneeling and fi ring his submachine gun. Near me, a compañero named Emilio Albentosa was walking toward the cane fi eld. A burst of gunfi re hit us both. I felt a sharp blow on my chest and a wound in my neck, and I thought for certain I was dead. Albentosa, vomiting blood and bleeding profusely from a deep wound made by a .45-caliber bullet, shouted: 'They've killed me' and began to fi re his rifl e at no one in particular" (Deutschmann 1997:26).

W hile he was lying alone on the ground waiting to die, Guevara was approached by one of members of the group who urged him to get up and go with him into the nearby cane fi eld, where they encountered two other men. According to Guevara's account of this situation: "[Juan] Almeida approached, urging me to go on, and despite the intense pain I dragged myself into the cane fi eld. . . . Then everything became a blur of airplanes fl ying low and strafi ng the fi eld. . . . With Almeida leading, we crossed the last path among the rows of cane and reached the safety of the woods. The fi rst shouts of 'Fire' were heard in the cane fi eld and columns of fl ame and smoke began to rise. . . . We walked until the darkness made it impossible to go on, and decided to lie down and go to sleep all huddled together in a heap. We were starving and thirsty, and the mosquitoes added to our misery. This was our baptism of fi re on December 5, 1956, in the outskirts of Niquero. Such was the beginning of forging what would become the Rebel Army" (page 27).

Meanwhile back in Mexico, Hilda and Hildita had moved out of their apartment and into the home of one of Hilda's friends. According to the plans she and Che had made before his departure, as soon as she saw news of the expedition's invasion of Cuba in the newspapers she and Hildita were to leave for Peru, where they would await the outcome of the revolutionary struggle. If this struggle succeeded, they were to join him in Cuba, stay there for a while, and "then decide whether to go to Peru or Argentina to continue the fi ght," since it was "Che's intention to continue fi ghting in other countries of Latin America" (Gadea 2008:208).

O n December 2, 1956, the news of Fidel Castro's expedition was published in all the Mexico City newspapers. The fi rst headline Hilda saw read " Invasion of Cuba by Boat— Fidel Castro, Ernesto Guevara, Raul Castro and all other members of the expedition dead " (page 209). She was shocked and overwhelmed with grief, but some of her friends cautioned her to wait for confi rmation of this bad news; they said both the Cuban and Mexican government authorities were most likely spreading false information to the press to discourage people from supporting Castro's cause. General Bayo visited Hilda and told her he didn't believe what the newspapers were reporting. In fact, he told her he was sure Guevara was alive. He said: "I can tell you this: he's the most intelligent, the cleverest—the one who most profi ted from my instruction. I am sure nothing has happened to him" (page 210).

Then Guevara's father called Hilda from Argentina to say he had contacted one of his cousins, who was the Argentine ambassador in Cuba. He said his cousin told him his son was not among the dead, the wounded, or the prisoners taken by the Cuban authorities. Still not knowing for sure whether he was alive or dead, Hilda followed the plan they had made before the departure of the expedition. She left Mexico with Hildita to go stay with her parents in Lima, Peru. Bur after staying there for a few weeks, they both went to Argentina at the invitation of Guevara's parents. Just before they left for Argentina, she received a call from his father, who informed her they had received word that Ernesto was alive.

The fi rst letter that Hilda received from Guevara was dated January 28, 1957 (Gadea 2008:216). It provides an excellent summary of his baptism of fi re and his fi rst days on Cuban soil. In this letter, he wrote: "As you probably know, after seven days of being packed like sardines in the now famous *Granma,* we landed at a dense, rotting mangrove jungle through the pilot's error. Our misfortunes continued until fi nally we were surprised in the also now famous Alegría [de Pío] and scattered like pigeons." He said he had been wounded in the neck, but he survived "due to my cat's lives." He explained to her that "a machine-gun bullet hit a cartridge case in my chest pocket, and the bullet ricocheted and nicked my neck. For a few days I walked through those hills thinking I was seriously wounded because the bullet had banged my chest so hard." He also described in this letter how his group managed to survive:

"Our group, including Almeida and Ramirito, whom you know, spent seven days of hunger and terrible thirst until we were able to slip through the cordon and, with help from the peasants, get back to rejoin Fidel."

What he undoubtedly knew (but did not want to reveal to his wife) when he wrote this letter was that of the 82 members of the *Granma* expedition, most were killed or caught and then murdered by the Cuban army in the fi rst days after the guerrilla force landed in Oriente Province. Besides Guevara and the Castro brothers, there were only 12 other survivors. As he hinted in his letter to Hilda, among those who were killed was Ñico López, his friend since Guatemala days.

T he survivors of the *Granma* expedition were joined by six discontented peasants in January 1957, and this minuscule group began operating as a guerrilla force from hiding places in the Sierra Maestra. Their fi rst victory was an attack on a small army garrison on the coast where the La Plata River comes down out of the Sierra Maestra to the ocean. As Guevara later wrote about this attack: "The effect of our victory was electrifying and went far beyond that craggy region. It was like a clarion call, proving that the Rebel Army really existed and was ready to fi ght" (Deutschmann 1997:28). At this time, they had only 22 weapons and they were short of ammunition. He wrote they had to take the garrison "at all costs, for a failure would have meant expending all our ammunition, leaving us practically defenseless."

O n January 16, 1957, they observed the garrison from the distance and took prisoner the drunken foreman of a local plantation who gave them information about the garrison. Under the cover of darkness, they attacked the garrison's small buildings from the left, center, and right.

Guevara was in the group that attacked from the center. At great risk and under heavy fi re, he and another man got close enough to set one of the three buildings on fi re. Intimidated by the fi re, the soldiers gave up the fi ght and surrendered. As a result, the guerrillas were able to seize their weapons, ammunition, fuel, food, and clothing. While none of the guerrillas received even a scratch in the fi ghting, they killed two of the soldiers, wounded fi ve, and took three prisoners. The rest of the soldiers fl ed into the night. After attending to the wounded, the guerrillas set fi re to the barracks and withdrew into the Sierra Maestra (page 32).

A ccording to Guevara, their humane treatment of prisoners "was in open contrast to that of Batista's army." He wrote: "Not only did they kill our wounded; they abandoned their own. This difference made a great impact on the enemy over time and it was a factor in our victory."

A s the months went by, the guerrillas carried out a number of daring attacks against small military outposts in the region. They were able to do this with the help they received from the 26th of July Movement's clandestine urban network of supporters in Santiago de Cuba led by Frank País and Celia Sánchez. This network sent men, arms, ammunition, and food to the Rebel Army. Castro assigned Guevara to be the liaison between this urban underground network and the guerrilla force. In March 1957, Guevara guided a group of over 50 men that Frank País had recruited and sent to join the guerrilla force in the Sierra Maestra.

By April 1957, the guerrilla force totaled some 80 men.

T he news of their actions began to attract the support of local peasants and the members of other political groups that were opposed to the Batista dictatorship all over the country. The ranks of the guerrilla force began to swell with recruits from these groups, the local peasantry, and the urban supporters of the 26th of July Movement in the cities of Santiago, Bayamo, Guantánamo, and Manzanillo.

Guevara was to have been the medical offi cer of the revolutionary guerrilla force, but his value as a guerrilla leader soon became evident. According to Fidel Castro, Che distinguished himself and won the admiration of his comrades at the second encounter their small guerrilla force had with the army on May 28, 1957. This battle took place in El Uvero, a small village along the road from Niquero to Santiago de Cuba.

In this battle, the guerrillas actually outnumbered the army by 80 to 53 (Bonachea and San Martín 1974:95). They took the army unit by surprise, and in an exchange of gunfi re that lasted almost three hours, they killed 14 soldiers and wounded 19 before the remaining soldiers surrendered. Their own losses were 7 dead and 9 wounded. Guevara considered this battle to be one of the most important of the revolutionary war. He wrote later that "for us, it was a victory that meant our guerrillas had reached full maturity. From this moment on, our morale increased enormously, our determination and hope for victory also increased, and though the months that followed were a hard test, we now had the key to the secret of how to beat the enemy" (Guevara 1963:72). Using the element of surprise, they were now strong enough to encircle most enemy units and force them to surrender or fl ee under the threat of complete annihilation.

A. ccording to Guevara, after El Uvero "the relationship of forces in the Sierra Maestra began to shift greatly" in favor of the Rebel rmy, and the government's forced evacuation of peasants from the area resulted "in a thousand crimes, robberies, and abuses against them." However, as he noted, "the peasants responded with renewed support to the cause of the July 26 Movement" and the guerrilla's "fair treatment toward the peasantry—respecting their property, paying for what we consumed, tending their sick, helping those most in need—was the total opposite of the government's bestial policy."

B. y this point, Guevara's bravery and military prowess had impressed and won over his Cuban comrades. As Castro later wrote: "From the very fi rst moment, he was absolutely willing to give his life, regardless of whether it was in the fi rst battle or the second or the third. Here we had a person born in a place thousands of kilometers from our country . . . but for that country and that cause, he was the fi rst at every moment to volunteer for something dangerous, for a mission with great risks" (page 105). Castro described Guevara's role in El Uvero as follows: "In a practically individual battle with an enemy soldier, in the midst of general combat, he shot the adversary and crawled forward under a hail of bullets to take his weapon . . . and it earned him the admiration of all" (Deutschmann 1994:102).

A ccording to Castro: "Che was one of those people who was liked immediately, for his simplicity, his character, his naturalness, his comradely attitude, his personality, his originality, even when one had not yet learned of his other unique qualities" (Castro 1994:68). Initially, as the guerrilla force's only doctor, he established a special bond with the other members of the small force. But in the force's second victorious battle, as Castro has stated, he became "the most outstanding soldier in that battle, carrying out for the fi rst time one of those singular feats that characterized him in all military action" (page 69). In subsequent battles, according to Castro, he was outstanding as both combatant and doctor, caring for wounded comrades as well as wounded enemy soldiers.

In one case during the early months of the guerrilla force's campaign in the Sierra Maestra, Guevara stayed behind with the wounded after the rest of force abandoned the scene of a bloody encounter with the army. Castro's account of this occasion is as follows: "After all the weapons had been captured and it became necessary to abandon that position, undertaking a long return march under the harassment of various enemy forces, someone had to stay behind with the wounded, and it was Che who did so. Aided by a small group of our soldiers, he took care of them, saved their lives, and later rejoined the column with them" (page 70). As Castro's account reveals: "From this time forward, he stood out as a capable and valiant leader, one of those who, when a diffi cult mission is pending, do not wait to be asked to carry it out." Indeed, his willingness to instantly volunteer for the most diffi cult missions "aroused admiration—twice the usual admiration," according to Castro, since he "was so altruistic, so selfl ess, so willing to always do the most diffi cult things" and "to constantly risk his life."

Because of how he distinguished himself in combat and because he had won the respect and admiration of his comrades, Castro gave Guevara increasingly greater military responsibilities. In March 1957, he appointed him, along with Ramiro Valdes, Ciro Redondo, and Camilo Cienfuegos, to the rank of captain. And a few months later, on July 21, 1957, Castro appointed Guevara as *comandante* (commander or major), the highest rank in the guerrilla army, which was held at the time only by Fidel Castro himself (page 70). In addition, Fidel placed Guevara at the head of a new guerrilla column with instructions to operate apart from the main force. It was called the Dispossessed Peasants and consisted of three platoons. This force numbered close to 75 men who, Guevara said, made him feel "very proud," despite their being "heterogeneously dressed and armed" (page 38).

Guevara's own account of how Castro appointed him commander and how he received his commander's star is worth noting here. In *Episodes of the Revolutionary War,* he wrote the following account: "We wrote a letter of congratulations and appreciation to 'Carlos,' the underground name of Frank País, who was living his fi nal days. It was signed by all the offi cers of the guerrilla army who knew how to write. (Many of the Sierra peasants were not very skilled in this art but were already an important component of the guerrillas.) The signatures appeared in two columns, and as we were writing down the ranks on the second one, when my turn came, Fidel simply said: 'Make it commander.' Thus, in a most informal manner, almost in passing, I was promoted to commander of the second column of the guerrilla army." Guevara also noted in this account: "There is a bit of vanity hiding somewhere within every one of us. It made me feel like the proudest man in the world that day." And he added: "My insignia, a small star, was given to me by Celia Sánchez," who was present on this important occasion (page 38). This star, which he wore on the front of his black beret, soon became an important feature of his now legendary iconic image.

A few days later, on July 30, 1957, Frank País, who was only 23 years old at the time, was killed by Batista's police as he left the house where he was hiding in Santiago. Unaware that País had been killed, the next day Guevara's column attacked a small army post in the Sierra Maestra town of Bueycito (Bonachea and San Martín 1974:96). In this attack, they again caught soldiers at a post by surprise and wounded six of them. However, one of the members of Guevara's column was killed and three others were wounded in the attack. As they left the town, one of the local miners decided to join them. He later became a well-known comandante in the Rebel Army.

When they returned to their base in the mountains, they heard the news of Frank País's death. Guevara later wrote that the death of País "represented an enormous loss to the Revolution," since he was "one of the purest, most brilliant fi gures of the Cuban Revolution." As a result of País's death, there were mass public protests in both Santiago and Havana, and the government responded with complete censorship of the press as well as the arrest and murder of a large number of the urban supporters of the 26th of July Movement. Guevara wrote: "When Frank País was murdered, we lost one of our most valuable fi ghters, but the people's reaction to the crime showed that additional forces were joining the struggle and the people's fi ghting spirit had increased" (Guevara 1963:96).

I n 1957 Guevara's column spent August in a small valley called El Hombrito near the summit of the Sierra Maestra. Since his column was composed of a large number of new recruits, they had to be trained, but they also had to be ready for battle at any moment. According to Guevara, it was their duty to attack any enemy units that dared invade what they called the "free territory of Cuba," which at this time was a relatively small section of the Sierra Maestra (page 97).

On August 29, a local peasant informed them that a large number of soldiers were headed their way on the trail that led to the valley where they were camped. Guevara had his men take up positions along the trail so they could ambush the soldiers when they reached a curve where the trail made an almost 90-degree turn around a rock. His plan was to let 10 or 12 soldiers go by the rock and then open fi re on them. His men were supposed to then take the dead soldiers' weapons and withdraw while they were being covered by their rear guard. However, when the soldiers came to the rock, one of his men opened fi re too soon and they succeeded in wounding only one of the soldiers at the head of the army column. Nevertheless, in the exchange of gunfi re that followed they managed to force the soldiers, who were equipped with bazookas, to retreat.

A s Guevara noted in his *Episodes of the Revolutionary War* (page 100), this encounter with a large army unit of some 180 men proved that it was relatively easy for the guerrillas to attack large enemy columns on the march, since they could ambush and fi re on the head of the enemy's approaching column and immobilize the rest of the column. In his account of this battle, Guevara wrote: "We continued this practice until it became an established system, so effi cient that the soldiers stopped coming to the Sierra Maestra and even refused to be part of the advance guard." He added that, "of course, it took more than one battle for our system to materialize." Moreover, he noted his guerrilla force was quite satisfi ed with these small victories at the time this battle took place, since they were still a poorly prepared, small guerrilla force that had only light weapons to confront well-equipped army units.

On November 4, 1957, the fi rst issue of *El Cubano Libre* (*The Free Cuban*) , the newspaper of the Rebel Army, was published by Guevara in the Sierra Maestra. The choice of this name for the newspaper had considerable historical signifi cance, since *El Cubano Libre* was the name of the paper published by Cuban patriots during the independence wars against Spanish colonialism in the 19th century. A few months later, Guevara was also instrumental in creating the Rebel Army's clandestine radio station Radio Rebelde, which began its transmissions in February 1958 by stating it was broadcasting from "the free territory of Cuba." Soon, Radio Rebelde began regularly broadcasting news of the Rebel Army's actions as well as the declarations of the 26th of July Movement, speeches by Castro, Cuban political news, and coded messages from the movement's members to their loved ones. It subsequently also provided radio communications between the rebel columns operating in different parts of the island.

G uevara was the main proponent of establishing this clandestine radio station. He had been impressed by the role that the CIA-backed radio station La Voz de la Liberación (The Voice of Liberation) had played in the overthrow of the Árbenz government in Guatemala (Moore 1993). Radio Rebelde, with its trademark salutation "Aquí Radio Rebelde" (Radio Rebelde here), still broadcasts today in Cuba.

D uring April and early May 1958, Castro had Guevara take charge of creating a training school for the new recruits that were joining the Rebel Army in increasing numbers. They were put through a lengthy political, physical, and military training program similar to the training the *Granma* group underwent in Mexico. Castro and Guevara wanted only the toughest and most dedicated recruits to join the Rebel Army, and they used the training program to weed out the weaker recruits.

Castro also gave Guevara the responsibility for defending the western sector of the territory held by the Rebel Army against the full-scale offensive launched against it by the Batista government's armed forces at the end of May 1958. This offensive was undertaken by a force of some 15,000 troops. They were armed with mortars and bazookas and supported by tanks and aircraft. Their strategy was to encircle and annihilate the Rebel Army. They divided into three combat battalions, which attacked Castro's guerrilla forces from three different directions. The guerrillas fell back to the defensive positions they had prepared in the Sierra Maestra and ambushed the army battalions as they tried to advance.

The fi ghting was intense, and the guerrillas had to give up much territory, but the government forces failed to defeat the Rebel Army. The government forces launched their last major attack on the Rebel Army on June 28, 1958, using two battalions of troops that were camped at the Estrada Palma Sugar Mill at the base of the Sierra Maestra (Bockman 1984). As these troops advanced into the mountain using a single road, they were attacked by units of the Rebel Army under Guevara's command when they had gone only a few miles. Guevara's units ambushed and pinned down the lead battalion, which called up armored cars to clear the way ahead of them. As the armored cars advanced, they ran into minefi elds Guevara's troops had planted on both sides of the road. Several armored cars were destroyed or disabled by the mines, and soldiers began to panic and retreat as they came under increasing sniper fi re from Guevara's sharpshooters.

The retreat of the troops in the fi rst battalion turned into a rout when they saw that the second battalion was not coming to their relief. As both of the army battalions withdrew in a disorganized manner, Guevara's guerrillas moved in on them from the sides and cut them to ribbons. In total, the army suffered 86 casualties, whereas Guevara's force had only 3 casualties. Guevara's force also captured a large number of weapons and 18,000 rounds of ammunition (Bockman 1984).

By mid-July 1958, the guerrilla forces of the Rebel Army had taken the initiative away from Batista's increasingly demoralized and battered troops. In fact, during the fi rst 11 days of combat in July, the guerrillas captured over 200 of Batista's soldiers, who were no match for the guerrilla fi ghters of the Rebel Army in the rugged terrain of the Sierra Maestra. By this point, it was clear the offensive was a failure and it became a tremendous propaganda victory for Castro's forces. Over 1,000 of the government's soldiers were killed, wounded, or taken prisoner. The Rebel Army turned over approximately 450 prisoners to the Red Cross. As Guevara later wrote: "Batista's army came out of that last offensive in the Sierra Maestra with its spine broken" (Deutschmann:51).

T he Battle of Las Mercedes at the end of July and the beginning of August 1958 was the last signifi cant battle of the Batista government's summer 1958 offensive against the Rebel Army (Bockman 1984). This battle started out as a trap designed to lure the columns under Castro's command into a place where they could be surrounded and destroyed by a much larger force. As the battle began, the Cuban army general in charge of the offensive called on special reinforcements that he had stationed nearby to move into the area and trap Castro's guerrilla columns

(Bockman 1984). The reinforcements, a force of some 1,500 troops, started heading toward the area where Castro's columns were engaged in Las Mercedes with other units under the general's command. Castro realized his forces were in a precarious position, and he called on Guevara's column to come to their aid.

Guevara had the ability to see in his mind's eye the whole battlefi eld in any given encounter. He quickly fi gured out the army's plan and saw that Castro's columns could be saved from disaster only if the army reinforcements heading toward the area were prevented from reaching the scene. As result, Guevara ordered his men to ambush these troops and keep them from reaching the scene of the battle. His men succeeded in blocking the advance of the army reinforcements. They infl icted serious casualties on the advancing troops and took about 50 prisoners. This action allowed Castro's columns to slip out of the trap set for them by the army. Years later, Major Larry Bockman of the U.S. Marine Corps Command and Staff College analyzed Guevara's tactics during this battle, and he concluded they were brilliant (Bockman 1984). The action taken by Guevara's column kept the Las Mercedes battle from resulting in Castro's death or capture by the government's forces.

H aving turned Batista's offensive into a guerrilla victory and a major propaganda success, the Rebel Army was able to attract widespread political support. On July 20, the leaders of the Cuban political parties opposing the Batista regime, both moderates and conservatives, signed a declaration in Caracas, called the Caracas Pact, in which they threw their support behind the 26th of July Movement and the Rebel Army.

N ow the Rebel Army went on the offensive with the strategy of carrying out a three-pronged attack on Santiago de Cuba in the east, the cities in Las Villas Province in the center of the country, and the province of Pinar del Rio at the western end of the island. The key to the success of this strategy was the campaign to divide the country in two by taking control of Las Villas Province. In August 1958, Castro gave Guevara instructions to lead two columns down from the Sierra Maestra to the plains of Camaguey and then march toward Las Villas, where they would cut the country in half and block the movement of troops from Havana to the eastern half of the island.

Guevara took the lead of one of the two columns and Camilo Cienfuegos headed the other. They took separate routes through Camaguey Province toward Las Villas. Cienfuegos's column headed for the northern portion of Las Villas with instructions to establish a base of operations around the small town of Yaguajay. From there, his column was to head toward Pinar del Rio at the western end of the island. Guevara's column had instructions to establish a base of operations in the Escambray Mountains in the southern portion of Las Villas. The mission of his column was to convince the various small guerrilla groups operating there to join forces with his column and tie down the government troops in the central portion of the island so they could not reinforce the army units that were being attacked by the Rebel Army's on two fronts (led by Fidel and Raúl Castro) in Oriente Province.

G uevara and his men made the march from the Sierra Maestra in Oriente Province on foot and on horses over diffi cult terrain, crossing fl ooded rivers and streams caused by a hurricane at the beginning of September. He described this march as follows: "Days of tiring marches through desolate expanses where there was only water and mud. We were hungry, thirsty and could hardly advance because our legs were as heavy as lead and the weapons were enormously heavy" (Deutschmann:53).

A s Guevara's column moved across the plains of Camaguey toward Las Villas, it was subjected to constant attacks from Batista's army and air force. Guevara wrote: "Despite the diffi culties we were never without the encouragement of the peasants," who served as their guides or gave them food, without which they could not have had the strength to go on (page 54). They escaped the ambushes and airstrikes and won one battle after another. Moreover, the almost suicidal character of their maneuvers against the regular army units they encountered seriously demoralized the government's forces. Meanwhile, Cienfuegos's column outmaneuvered and slipped past the army units in their path and made its way to Yaguajay.

Guevara's column made its way through Camaguey Province, and on October 16, 1958, they swam across the Júcaro River, which divides the provinces of Camaguey and Las Villas, in order to slip through the encirclement the army had set up to trap them. Within a few days, they arrived safely in the Escambray Mountains, thanks to the tactical skills and leadership provided by Guevara.

A. e convinced the fi ve groups of guerrillas already operating in the Es-cambray Mountains to join with his men in attacking the army garrisons in the center of the province. To achieve this objective, Guevara had to convince the leaders of these independent organizations to join forces with his column. In referring to this accomplishment, he later wrote: "After laborious talks I had with their respective leaders, we reached a series of agreements and it was possible to go on to form a more or less common front" (Deutschmann:57). This common front was an extremely important achievement in the struggle to create revolutionary unity among the various groups fi ghting the Batista government. From the Escambray Mountains, they were able to harass the Batista dictatorship's armed forces and their communications network in Las Villas Province.

In a desperate attempt to shore up his shaky regime, Batista tried to stage a rigged national election in November 1958. But Castro called on the population to abstain from participating in the elections and ordered his forces to disrupt the elections. The election was boycotted by a majority of the citizenry and by all the political parties that had signed the Caracas Pact. The public's repudiation of the rigged election so infuriated Batista that he launched an unprecedented reign of police terror against the general populace. The guerrillas took this as the cue to begin their general offensive to bring down the dictatorship.

I. t was in the Escambray Mountains that Guevara met Aleida March, whom he later married (after divorcing Hilda Gadea). March was a schoolteacher in Santa Clara who joined the local branch of the 26th of July Movement in 1956 (March 2008:37). She subsequently served as a clandestine arms courier, saboteur, and messenger for the movement throughout Las Villas Province. n late October 1958, the leadership of the movement in the province gave her money to take to Guevara's guerrilla force in the Escambray Mountains. She had orders to stay on with Guevara's force because it would be too dangerous for her to return to her previous activities.

I n her fi rst meeting with Guevara, she gave him 50,000 pesos that she had strapped to her body (page 59). She told him she had been ordered to place herself under his command because the Batista authorities were hunting for her and she knew too much about the movement's clandestine network to be captured by the authorities. At fi rst, Guevara refused to grant her request to join his column as a combatant and suggested she stay at the column's base camp as a nurse. She argued that she had spent the last two years working clandestinely for the movement and that this experience gave her the right to be a guerrilla fi ghter and not a nurse (pages 60–61). He compromised by asking her to serve as his personal secretary (page 71). After his column had fought its way across the province to the provincial capital in Santa Clara, he gave her an M1 rifl e and told her she had earned it. This gesture made her feel that he regarded her as a true combatant—no different in this respect than any of the other members of his column (page 85).

During November and December 1958, Guevara's column and Cienfuegos's column, aided by their allies from the Escambray Mountains, carried out a series of lightning attacks that captured most of the towns, closed the highways, and blocked the railroad lines throughout Las Villas Province. Although they were subjected to constant aerial attacks from Batista's air force and they often faced much larger forces with tanks and heavy weapons, they managed to outmaneuver, demoralize, and defeat their opponents in almost every encounter. As a result of their successful campaign to rapidly seize most of the towns and strategic points in the province, they ended up in control of over 3,000 square miles of territory in a period of a few weeks, and they prevented the government from sending troops to Oriente Province except by air and sea.

They followed a strategy of launching surprise attacks on the garrisons of the army and Rural Guard units in the towns and smaller cities of the province. They would surround barracks or forts and then force them to surrender after cutting off their supplies and threatening to set fi re to, or in some cases actually setting fi re to, the buildings government forces occupied. The guerrillas promised to release them after they surrendered if they would hand over all their weapons and ammunition, would listen to a lecture about the goals of the revolution, and agreed to leave the province immediately. In some cases, the guerrillas released them to the Red Cross, which then escorted them out of the province. As the news of these surrenders spread throughout the province, the local population offered them increasing support and assistance.

A t the end of December 1958, the decisive battle of the revolutionary war was fought by Guevara's column and his allies in Santa Clara, the largest city in Las Villas Province. Santa Clara was the transportation and communications hub of Las Villas and possessed approximately 150,000 inhabitants at the time. It had a railroad station, an airport, and television and radio stations.

G uevara's force, outnumbered nine to one, faced a force of some 3,200 soldiers, Rural Guards, and police (Taibo 1996:304). This force had superior weaponry (tanks, armored personnel carriers, mortars, bazookas, canons, and an armored train), was supported by the air force, and occupied the hills surrounding the city as well as its tallest buildings. Guevara, on the other hand, had a force under his command that totaled only 214 combatants. They were organized into seven platoons with light weapons. The heaviest weapons they possessed were .30-caliber machine guns. They did have one bazooka, but they did not have any rockets for it. In fact, they were low on ammunition and had had very little sleep, since they had been fi ghting constantly over the preceding 10 days.

O n the night of December 27, 1958, the advance unit of Guevara's force arrived at the outskirts of the city. They were followed by a convoy of confi scated trucks and jeeps fi lled with Guevara's experienced guerrillas from the Sierra Maestra, the guerrillas of the rebel organization called the Revolutionary Directorate, which had joined forces with him in the Escambray Mountains, and new recruits (students and peasants) who had been recently trained at Guevara's base camp in the mountains. The convoy took a little used back road that brought them to the provincial university campus on the edge of the city. Guevara initially established his command center there and later moved it into the center. On the 28th, he sent his units to capture strategic points in the city while the Revolutionary Directorate's units laid siege to the garrison of the Rural Guards.

A leida March was constantly at Guevara's side. She knew the city's street pattern well and was able to guide him and his men through the city as they attacked one after another of the positions held by the army units and the police defending the city. She also was able to help him gain support from the local population. As they moved toward the center of Santa Clara, they often had to dodge bullets as they ran from building to building (March:85). Both of them later recalled how frightened they were the other one would be harmed when at one particularly dangerous moment they had to run across a street in front of an army tank that was shooting in their direction.

G uevara was concerned about both the army units stationed on a hill called El Cápiro overlooking the city and the armored train with some 400 soldiers and heavy weapons that was stationed on the railway tracks below them. Thus, the units on the hill and the armored train were strategic targets for Guevara's units. He had his men bring a bulldozer from the school of agronomy at the university to remove 30 feet of rails from the railway line so that the train would be derailed if it attempted to move from its position below the hill.

Guevara ordered his suicide squad, led by 18-year-old Roberto Rodríguez—nicknamed the "Cowboy Kid"—to capture the hill. They succeeded in dislodging the soldiers from the hill and started to attack the train, which withdrew toward the middle of town in the direction where the rails had been removed. As Guevara planned, the train was derailed as it attempted to fl ee with its cargo of troops, weapons, and ammunition. According to his account, at this point "a very interesting battle ensued: the men in the armored train had been dislodged by our Molotov cocktails [but] in spite of their excellent protection they were prepared to fi ght only at long range. . . . Harassed by our men who from nearby train carriages and other close-range positions were hurling bottles of fl aming gasoline, the train—thanks to its armor plate—became a veritable oven for its soldiers. After several hours, the entire crew surrendered, with their twenty-two armored cars, their anti-aircraft guns, their DCA machine guns, and their fabulous quantities of ammunition (fabulous, that is, to us)" (Guevara 1968:252). Actually, Guevara's account is too modest since it was he who personally negotiated the surrender of the soldiers on the train by meeting unarmed with their commander and assuring them he would allow them to return to Havana escorted by the Red Cross after they laid down their arms (Taibo:244).

A s word went through the city of the surrender of the troops on the train, the citizenry began barricading the streets with cars and buses in order to obstruct the movement of the army's tanks and armored cars. Batista ordered the air force to bomb and strafe the city, which it did repeatedly. But even though many buildings were reduced to rubble and the civilian population was terrorized by the air force's indiscriminate bombing and strafi ng of the city, the situation could not be reversed.

A. fter the troops on the train surrendered, the large number of police and four army tanks that were defending the main police station were persuaded to surrender by one of Guevara's offi cers. In the fi ghting leading up to the surrender of the police station, the Cowboy Kid was killed. The Rural Guards garrison capitulated to the Revolutionary Directorate fi ghters with the aid of some of Guevara's units which used some of the heavy weapons confi scated from the armored train, and then, according to Guevara: "The prison, the courthouse, and the provincial government headquarters fell to us, as well as the Grand Hotel where the besieged men continued their fi re from the tenth fl oor almost until the cessation of hostilities" (page 253).

B. y New Year's Day 1959, Guevara's forces had gained control of the city except for some 1,000 soldiers inside the Leoncio Vidal Army Garrison, the largest military installation in central Cuba. Guevara had been concerned they might attempt to mount a counterattack on his forces, and he had directed most of his units to concentrate on the garrison and begin to assault it. However, as the news of the surrenders in Santa Clara reached Havana, the dictator atista and his immediate family fl ed the country. Informed of this, the commander of the garrison contacted Guevara about negotiating an indefi nite truce. After consulting with Castro, Guevara met with the commander of the garrison and told him the following: "It's either unconditional surrender or fi re, but real fi re, and with no quarter. The city is already in our hands. At 12:30 p.m. I will give the order to resume the attack using all our forces. We will take the barracks at all costs. You will be responsible for the bloodshed" (Taibo:253). The commander went back to talk to his offi cers, but the soldiers were already deserting their positions and fraternizing with Guevara's men. They began to throw their weapons down and walk unarmed over to the rebel lines. The battle for Santa Clara was over. Guevara's troops allowed the surrendered soldiers to leave Santa Clara unarmed and return to Havana via the port city of Caibarién.

Over Radio Rebelde, Castro demanded the surrender of the besieged garrison in Santiago and he ordered Guevara and Cienfuegos to march their columns immediately to Havana. He gave Guevara orders to take over La Cabaña fortress, which dominates the entrance to Havana and its harbor, and he gave Cienfuegos orders to occupy the Camp Columbia barracks, which was the most important garrison of Batista's army. On January 2, 1959, they left in a convoy of trucks and jeeps for Havana. On the way to Havana, Guevara made his fi rst declaration of love for Aleida when the convoy stopped for gas and they found themselves alone for a moment. He told her that he realized he was in love with her in Santa Clara when they had to cross the street almost directly in front of the tank that was fi ring in their direction. He told her he couldn't bear the thought of something happening to her (March 2008:85).

I n the early morning hours of January 3, 1959, Guevara and Cienfuegos arrived with their columns in Havana. According to Aleida's account of their arrival at the imposing La Cabaña fortress overlooking the city: "In such a fortress it was strange to observe how the mass of soldiers subordinated themselves to the rebel command without any kind of opposition. This fact revealed a great deal about the moral breakdown of the dictatorship, but above all else about the trust and respect for the new Rebel Army, which had the unconditional support of the people" (page 95).

Meanwhile, Castro marched with his troops to Santiago de Cuba to capture the Moncada, the fortress where he had made an abortive attempt six years earlier to bring down the Batista regime. On January 5, fi ve Latin American countries recognized Castro's provisional government. Great Britain and a number of other nations soon followed. On January 7, the United States recognized the new government, and recalled Ambassador Earl Smith, who was unanimously condemned by Cuban public opinion for having supported Batista. On January 8, Castro's column arrived in Havana, where Guevara and Cienfuegos awaited him.

As Fidel triumphantly rode into the city, his brother Raúl was at his right and Guevara was at his left. In less than three years, the young Argentine had risen from the obscure existence of a roving young adventurer to become one of the most popular and important leaders in the Cuban Revolution. Three years earlier he had only begun to think seriously about his political convictions and commitments, but now, at the age of 31, he found himself an accomplished military commander and one of the three most powerful leaders in the new government of Cuba.

While historical circumstances, destiny, or fate—call it what you will—must be given some of the credit for Guevara's meteoric rise to fame and power, the importance of the man's personality must not be underrated. By the time he arrived in Havana, Che seems to have acquired all the characteristics of a true revolutionary and charismatic leader. He demonstrated an amazing capacity for personal sacrifi ce, and he never compromised his ideals. From the time he became a guerrilla, he appears to have lived according to the motto *todo o nada* (all or nothing). In fact, he was so demanding of himself that he did not permit himself a single indulgence. This, of course, made it possible for him to demand a great deal from those around him.

C he had that quality of personal magnetism that attracts and inspires the loyalty and devotion of others. In the Sierra Maestra, his bravery, boldness, and determination invoked the enthusiasm of his comrades, and it soon became clear to Castro that Guevara was a natural leader. Once having elevated him to a position of leadership, Castro found that Che was an extremely capable and resourceful military commander. He gave him increasingly greater responsibilities, and in the end entrusted him with the most important and crucial campaign of the revolutionary war.

Castro had complete confi dence in Guevara, since he knew that he had no personal political ambitions. He recognized that as an Argentine, Guevara felt it was not his place to question the basic political objectives chosen by his Cuban comrades. Castro knew that he could count on Guevara's loyalty and unquestioning devotion to the goals of the revolutionary movement. Their relationship was very close, largely because of the similarity of their thinking, and he soon gave Guevara some of the most important positions of leadership in the new revolutionary regime.

CHAPTER SIX

Che's role in Cuba's Revolutionary Government

W hen the 26th of July Movement and its allies seized political power in January 1959, they quickly formed a new revolutionary government in Havana. It was led by a coalition of the top leaders of the revolutionary insurrection, Fidel Castro as well as prominent political fi gures who had opposed the Batista dictatorship but had not taken part in the revolutionary armed struggle that overthrew it. This new coalition government suffered a series of strains and internal confl icts almost immediately. Within a short time, Fidel Castro, other key revolutionary leaders, and the more militant supporters of the 26th of July Movement gained fi rm control over both the new government and the post-insurrectionary political situation in the country.

T he fortress of La Cabaña, which overlooks Old Havana and was occupied under the command of Che Guevara, soon became one of the bastions of the new revolutionary regime, and "El Che" almost overnight became one of the regime's most capable and charismatic leaders. He immediately transformed the La Cabaña fortress into a large training school for the men under his command, and he established a series of small factories in the huge fortress like those he had created in the Sierra Maestra (March 2008:99).

He told Aleida and his closest companions that although the insurrectionary war against the Batista dictatorship had ended, the real revolution had just begun, along with a new life for everyone involved. He said their task was to reestablish order out of chaos and organize themselves to accomplish this task. He began to dictate notes to Aleida about the tasks of the Rebel Army as the vanguard of the revolution, and she assumed the duties of his personal secretary.

CHE AND THE REVOLUTIONARY TRIBUNALS

D uring January 1959 the Rebel Army organized a series of revolutionary tribunals in La Cabaña that were held to publicly prosecute and punish the torturers, thugs, and murderers of the Batista dictatorship. A commission headed by a captain of the Rebel Army who had been a lawyer took responsibility for investigating and prosecuting government offi cials, members of the armed forces, and police accused by the public of the worst crimes and abuses under the Batista dictatorship.

A lthough Guevara, as the garrison commander of La Cabaña, received some of the appeals and interviewed some of the family members who pleaded for clemency in the case of some of the prisoners, he did not participate in any of the trials or the executions (March:101).

Nevertheless, the U.S. government and news media, and later the Cuban exile community in Miami (many of whom were sympathizers or former offi cials of the Batista dictatorship), accused Guevara of being in charge of the trials and executions since many of them took place in La Cabaña (Taibo:344). As time went by, the leaders of the Cuban exile community in Miami conducted a slanderous campaign to smear the popular image of Che by calling him "the Butcher of La Cabaña."

I n response to the U.S. campaign against the revolutionary tribunals, Fidel Castro launched a media counterattack on January 21, 1959, in which he compared the revolutionary tribunals with the famous Nuremberg trials held by the U.S. military at the end of World War II in Germany to punish top Nazi leaders and offi cials for the war crimes and crimes against humanity they had committed in Europe. Castro said the nature of the crimes committed by members of the Batista army and police was no different than that of those committed by the Nazis during their reign of terror in Europe, and thus the revolutionary tribunals in Cuba and execution by fi ring squad of the torturers and murderers of the Batista regime were a legitimate form of popular justice (Taibo:344).

T elevision, radio, magazines, and newspapers throughout Cuba were fi lled with accounts of the horrible acts of torture, rape, and murder committed by Batista military and police offi cials; the discovery of secret graves with the mutilated bodies of young men and women taken prisoner by the Batista authorities; and the testimonials of eyewitnesses to the massacres of peasants carried out by the Batista forces during the offensives against the Rebel Army in the Sierra Maestra (page 343). A private national survey carried out at this time in Cuba indicated that over

90 percent of the respondents supported the trials and the executions (page 343).

CHE'S MOTHER AND FATHER VISIT CUBA

On January 18, 1959, Guevara's mother and father arrived from Argentina. He met them at the airport with Aleida and his bodyguard. When his father asked who Aleida was, he told him she was the woman he was going to marry. A few days later, on January 21, Hilda Gadea and Che's three-year-old daughter, Hildita, arrived and were met by one of their mutual friends from their days together in Mexico City. When Gadea met Che, she said: "Ernesto, with his frankness of always, told me he had another woman that he had met in the battle for Santa Clara" (Gadea 2008:179; Taibo 344 – 45). She agreed to a divorce so that he could marry Aleida. She also decided to remain in Cuba so that Hildita could be educated there and spend time with her father. Shortly afterward, the new government publicly proclaimed Che Guevara to be a Cuban citizen with the same rights as every citizen born in Cuba.

O n May 17, 1959, Prime Minister Castro put into effect a new agrarianreform law, which allowed the government to take over Cuba's large estates and give them to the formerly landless peasants who worked them, but through the creation of a form of collective rather than individual private ownership. This was immediately denounced by top government offi cials in the United States and the media there as a dangerous threat to the private ownership of property in Cuba, particularly the large landholdings of U.S. citizens and companies. As a consequence, the value of shares in Cuba's U.S.-owned sugar companies dropped to an all-time

low on the New York Stock Exchange, and relations between the U.S. government and the new Cuban government became quite hostile. Signifi cantly, Che played an important role in the agrarian reform and the Cuban government's seizure of U.S.-owned companies.

CHE BECOMES CLOSE CONFIDANT OF FIDEL CASTRO

During the fi rst six months of the new government, Che became one of Fidel Castro's closest confi dants and advisers. On June 2, 1959, he married Aleida March. She continued to serve as his personal secretary, and she accompanied him nearly everywhere he went in Cuba. However, he refused to take her on a two-month-long international trip he undertook only two weeks after their wedding. He told her he could not take her with him because she was now his wife and it would not be fair to the others accompanying him on the trip who were not able to bring their partners with them.

O n June 12, 1959, Guevara left Cuba for the fi rst time since his arrival three years earlier on the *Granma*. The purpose of the trip was to establish friendly relations between the new government in Cuba and the governments of socialist Yugoslavia, the Arab states in the Middle East, and various countries in Asia. He had suggested this trip to Castro in May because he felt it was important for Cuba to establish close relations with the governments of these countries as soon as possible. Castro agreed with him that it was important to strengthen Cuba's relations with these countries. They both felt that in the event of U.S. military aggression against the new revolutionary regime the support of these countries would be decisive in gaining a favorable response from the General Assembly of the United Nations. In addition, they both thought close relations with these countries would permit Cuba's leaders to consult and collaborate with some of the most capable and important statesmen in the world at the time—internationally famous leaders such as Joseph Tito of Yugoslavia, Abdel Nasser of Egypt, Ahmed Ben Bella of Algeria, Jawaharlal Nehru of India, and Mao Tse-tung of the People's Republic of China. Indeed, during this trip Guevara met all of these leaders.

Castro trusted Che with this important mission and subsequent missions of a similar nature because he was confi dent Che would be an effective representative of Cuba's new revolutionary government. Over the next few years, these missions became one of Guevara's most important responsibilities, and they contributed greatly to the survival and international infl uence of Cuba's revolutionary regime.

G uevara returned to Cuba in August 1959. Shortly after his return, Castro presided over a meeting of the new National Institute of Agrarian Reform (its acronym in Spanish was INRA) and announced that he was appointing Guevara as head of the Department of Industrialization in that organization. As Guevara saw it, the new government's fi rst big battle to transform Cuba's neocolonial economy was the agrarian-reform program. This program confi scated the *latifundia* (big estates) in Cuba in order to give free land to the country's large number of poor peasants, made up of sharecroppers, tenant farmers, squatters, and small-scale sugarcane growers who had previously rented small plots of land. Later (1961), Che was appointed Minister of Industry.

Castro wanted Guevara to lead the effort to persuade the peasantry to increase the country's agricultural production so that it could fi nance the industrialization of the economy. He believed Guevara was the right person to do this since he had acquired a great deal of experience working closely with the peasantry during the guerrilla war against the Batista dictatorship. Moreover, he had been responsible for the small industries established in the Sierra Maestra by the Rebel Army that produced soap, boots, land mines, and other basic items needed by its members.

CHE TAKES CHARGE OF THE INDUSTRIALIZATION OF CUBA

As head of INRA's Department of Industrialization, Guevara became responsible for the increasing number of industries that were taken over by the revolutionary government, including the petroleum, nickel, sugarrefi ning, and tobacco industries. He also was responsible for developing the fi rst plans for the industrialization of the country, with the fundamental goal of creating industrial enterprises that would save the country valuable foreign exchange earnings by producing necessary products that previously had to be imported from abroad.

According to his wife, Aleida: "One of the most emotional moments of this stage was when Che had contact for the fi rst time with the miners and learned the extent of exploitation to which they had been submitted in the years of the neocolony, during which time their standard of life was exceedingly low in spite of the enormous effort they made, their nutrition was scarce and they didn't have any schooling." In her book about their life, she recounts how Che made sure "measures were taken to humanize not only their work, but also to dignify these human beings." She said, right from the start, "they were given an adequate diet, and workers dining halls and decorous housing" (March 2008:123).

A t the end of November 1959, Castro appointed Guevara to the important post of president of the Central Bank of Cuba, which placed him in charge of the country's fi nancial affairs. Shortly after Guevara assumed this position, he made a public declaration in which he said Cuba would not give any special guarantees to foreign corporations and that the country would seek close trade and fi nancial ties with the then existing socialist bloc of countries led by the Soviet Union.

Throughout the early sixties, Guevara became second only to Raúl Castro in his proximity to Fidel Castro and was Cuba's unoffi cial foreign relations minister (Guevara 2001:xiv). In addition to his political responsibilities, he wrote what has now become a classic work on revolutionary guerrilla warfare, *La Guerra de Guerrillas* (Guerrilla Warfare) (Guevara 1961), plus books and articles on various other subjects. One of the most famous of these books was *Reminiscences of the Cuban Revolutionary War* (Guevara 1968).

CHE'S ROLE IN SHAPING REVOLUTIONARY CUBA'S FOREIGN RELATIONS

C he played a major role in shaping the new Cuban government's relations with socialist countries, Latin American countries, the United States, and the newly independent nations in Africa, Asia, and the Middle East. He also played a major role in the secret negotiations that took place between the government of the Soviet Union and the Cuban government that allowed the Soviet Union to station nuclear missiles in Cuba (Anderson 1997:526–28). This fateful decision led to the infamous Cuban Missile Crisis of October 1962, in which the United States threatened the Soviet Union with nuclear war if it did not remove all its missiles from Cuba. This crisis brought the world closer to a devastating intercontinental nuclear war than any other incident during the four decades of the cold war between the United States and the Soviet Union.

C he also played a key role in placing Cuba at the forefront of what became known as the Third World, a loose anti-imperialist coalition of African, Asian, Middle Eastern, and Latin American countries—most of which had been previously conquered and colonized by one or more of the major Western countries. The political leaders of these Third World countries sought to increase their national independence and socioeconomic development by steering a middle course between the First World industrial-capitalist countries headed by the United States and the Second World socialist countries headed by the Soviet Union.

C he's speech at the United Nations in December 1964 provides an excellent example of the role he played in projecting Cuba's solidarity with Third World countries. In early December 1964, he traveled to New York City as head of the Cuban delegation to the United Nations General Assembly. While he was in New York he became an instant celebrity. For example, he appeared on the CBS Sunday news program *Face the Nation* and was invited by Malcolm X, one of the most famous African American political activists at the time, to appear with him at an important public rally in Harlem. Although Che was not able to attend this event in person, he sent Malcolm X a letter to read to the participants. Before Malcolm X read the letter, he told the crowd how much he admired Guevara, who he said was "one of the most revolutionary men in this country right now" (Anderson 1997:618).

I n Che's speech to the General Assembly entitled, "Colonialism is doomed," he vociferously denounced the United States as an imperialist and warmongering world power. He particularly condemned the U.S. government's military involvement in Vietnam, Cambodia, and Laos and the imperialist role he said the U.S. government was playing in Africa through its military intervention and support of neocolonial leaders in the Congo and its backing of the white racist regime in South Africa.

T he following is an excerpt from his speech to the General Assembly on December 11, 1964 (Deutschmann 1997:283–84):

Of all the burning problems to be dealt with by this Assembly, one of special signifi cance for us, and one whose solution we feel must be found fi rst—so as to leave no doubt in the minds of anyone—is that of peaceful coexistence among states with different economic and social systems. Much progress has been made in the world in this fi eld. But imperialism, particularly U.S. imperialism, has attempted to make the world believe that peaceful coexistence is the exclusive right of the earth's great powers. . . . At present, the type of peaceful coexistence to which we aspire is often violated. Merely because the Kingdom of Cambodia maintained a neutral attitude and did not bow to the machinations of U.S. imperialism, it has been subjected to all kinds of treacherous and brutal attacks from the Yankee bases in South Vietnam. Laos, a divided country, has also been the object of imperialist aggression of every kind. Its people have been massacred from the air. The conventions concluded at Geneva have been violated, and part of its territory is in constant danger of cowardly attacks by imperialist forces. The Democratic Republic of Vietnam knows all these histories of aggression as do few nations on earth. It has once again seen its frontier violated, has seen enemy bombers and fi ghter planes attack its installations and U.S. warships, violating territorial waters, attack its naval posts. At this time, the threat hangs over the Democratic Republic of Vietnam that the U.S. war makers may openly extend into its territory the war that for many years they have been waging against the people of South Vietnam.

Che made it clear in this speech that Cuba wanted to build socialism and it supported the socialist bloc of countries, but he said Cuba was also a member of the "nonaligned, Third World countries" because they were all fi ghting against imperialism to secure their national sovereignty. In this regard, he said:

W e want to build socialism. We have declared that we are supporters of those who strive for peace. We have declared ourselves to be within the group of Nonaligned countries, although we are Marxist-Leninists, because the Nonaligned countries, like ourselves, fi ght imperialism. We want peace. We want to build a better life for our people. That is why we avoid, insofar as possible, falling into the provocations manufactured by the Yankees. But we know the mentality of those who govern them. They want to make us pay a very high price for that peace.

A. e also made it clear that while Cuba rejected "accusations against us of interference in the internal affairs of other countries, we cannot deny that we sympathize with those people who strive for their freedom." And he stated that "we must fulfi ll the obligation of our government and people to state clearly and categorically to the world that we morally support and stand in solidarity with peoples who struggle anywhere in the world to make a reality of the rights of full sovereignty proclaimed in the UN Charter."

To most of those who knew and observed him during the years he served at Castro's side, Che was a model revolutionary leader. He was dedicated to his duties, absolutely convinced of the rightness of his cause, and devoted to Castro. In the opinion of many, he was the most intelligent and persuasive member of Castro's cabinet. But he was also clearly dissatisfi ed with the routine and bureaucratic aspects of his ministerial responsibilities. On a number of occasions he told his friends of his desire to return to the revolutionary armed struggle. As time went by, he spoke increasingly of the possibility of leaving his ministerial post and devoting his future efforts to the revolution against imperialism in Latin America and in other parts of the world.

C he's personal austerity and disregard for fl attery and personal gain presented a sharp contrast to the self-indulgent lifestyles, womanizing, and personal excesses of many of the people around him (Anderson 1997:571–72). In this regard, it is interesting to note that even though he was one of the most important and high-ranking members of the Cuban revolutionary government, he was famous for his careless appearance—he always wore his uniform shirt out of his pants and open at the throat and his boots were never laced to the top. Moreover, when he visited Cuba's industries, he always entered fi rst the workshops to talk with the workers, and only later would he go to the offi ces of the managers (Taibo 1996:467).

His casual dress and unconventional behavior can be traced to his vagabond trips around South America as a young man, when he seems to have taken delight in traveling for days without bathing or changing his clothes, and he was not distressed by traveling with little or no money or having no idea where he would stay the night. All of these traits helped him when he became a guerrilla fi ghter and he had to go without bathing, food, water, or a roof over his head.

Che had an ironic and sarcastic wit and a sharp tongue, but he could also laugh at himself. He practiced a curious blend of romanticism and pragmatism; and while he did demand a great deal of those around him, he demanded even more of himself (Anderson 1997:572).

In his lifestyle and personal conduct, he exemplifi ed the principles of individual sacrifi ce, honesty, loyalty, and dedication. Women were attracted to him, and he was constantly approached by people who wanted to do him favors, but he spurned all attempts at fl attery and pandering, hated brownnosers, and remained monogamous throughout his days in Cuba.

I. n the fall of 1960, Che was asked by a reporter from *Look* magazine if he was an orthodox Communist. His answer was no, he preferred to call himself a "pragmatic revolutionary." n fact, he was neither a pragmatic revolutionary nor an orthodox Communist. To be sure, his outlook, his values, and the events in which he participated generally placed him in the Communist ranks. But as *New York Times* correspondent Herbert Matthews said after interviewing him in 1960, Che would have had no emotional or intellectual problem in opposing the Communists if the circumstances had been otherwise (Matthews 1961).

He made common cause with most Communists because they were opposed to the same things in contemporary Latin American society he opposed. But Che differed from the more orthodox Communists, who tended to rigidly follow the ideological leadership and foreign policy goals of the Soviet Union. He particularly refused to accept their rigid ideological position that the proper conditions for a socialist revolution in Latin America and the rest of the Third World did not yet exist. Che fi rmly believed the Cuban Revolution demonstrated that socialist revolutions in the Third World could be launched successfully and without the direction and control of an orthodox Communist party. It was heretical views such as these that earned him the disfavor of the pro-Soviet and orthodox Communists.

C he's unorthodox political views and his distrust of the Soviet Union made him a prime target of the pro-Soviet Communists in Cuba. This group, led by Anibal Escalante, was in constant confl ict with Che right up to the time of his resignation from the cabinet in 1965. According to them, Cuba's economic instability and its strained relations with the Soviet Union were a direct result of Che's impractical projects and his "pathological" revolutionary adventurism.

T he assertion by this group that Che was a pathological adventurer must be discounted as an obvious attempt on their part to discredit a man who stood in the way of the policies advocated by this group of pro-Soviet Communists. Nevertheless, Che was a dreamer and an adventurer. He was prone to dreaming up grandiose plans and projects, especially when he was confi ned to bed by his asthma. One of his dreams was to lead a revolution in his native Argentina. And only a dreamer could have believed, as he did, that the revolutionary liberation of Latin America was an objective capable of realization in the mid-1960s.

As for the assertion that Che was an adventurer, this he admitted himself in his farewell letter to his parents (Gerassi 1968a:412), which he wrote in the spring of 1965, shortly before he departed Cuba on a secret mission to help the rebel forces in the Congo.

Dear Parents:

O nce again I feel below my heels the ribs of Rosinante [Don Quixote's scrawny horse]. I return to the road with my shield on my arm.

A lmost ten years ago, I wrote you another farewell letter. As I remember, I lamented not being a better soldier and a better doctor. The second doesn't interest me any longer. As a soldier I am not so bad.

Nothing in essence has changed, except that I am much more conscious, and my Marxism has taken root and become pure. I believe in the armed struggle as the only solution for those peoples who fi ght to free themselves, and I am consistent with my beliefs. Many will call me an adventurer, and that I am; only one of a different kind—one of those who risks his skin to prove his beliefs.

It could be that this may be the end. Not that I look for it, but it is within the logical calculus of probabilities. If it is so, I send you a last embrace. I have loved you very much, only I have not known how to express my love. I am extremely rigid in my actions and I believe that at times you did not understand me. It was not easy to understand me. On the other hand, I ask only that you believe in me today.

Now, a will that I have polished with the delight of an artist will sustain my pair of fl accid legs and tired lungs. I will do it!

R emember from time to time this little condottiere [Italian term for the captain of a band of soldiers of fortune] of the twentieth century. A kiss to Celia, to Roberto, Juan Martín and Pototín, to Beatriz, to everyone. A large embrace from your recalcitrant prodigal son.

Ernesto

Che knew full well that his life might well come to a violent end. In addition to his reference to this in his farewell letter to his parents in the spring of 1965, he also acknowledged the possibility in a letter that he sent at about the same time to his old friend and traveling partner Alberto Granados. In this letter he prophetically wrote: "My rolling house has two legs once again and my dreams will have no frontier—at least until the bullets speak."

C he was not a fanatic, and he did not have a pathological love of bloodshed or human cruelty. However, he was not a conventional and contented man. If he had been, he would never have become a revolutionary. He was a dreamer, an adventurer, and an unrelenting rebel against the established order of things. He was a man deeply incensed by the social injustices that he saw in the world all around him, and he was motivated by a sincere desire to rectify them.

He was the personifi cation of the true revolutionary—a superidealist who insists on bringing heaven immediately to earth. Moreover, his willingness to die for his ideals is proof that he possessed far more courage and conviction than the ordinary man or woman. Indeed, the fact that he fought and died for what he believed in makes him stand in sharp contrast to the vast majority of Latin America's political leaders, whose opportunism and lack of conviction have left the poor majority of the region's population with little hope that their condition will ever be improved by the existing political order.

CHAPTER SEVEN

Che's contribution to the revolutionary Guerrilla warfare

Che Guevara's ideas about revolution and guerrilla warfare are required reading for all those interested in understanding the nature of both topics. His book *La Guerra de Guerrillas* (*Guerrilla Warfare* in the 1985 English translation), which was fi rst published in 1961, is one of the most important publications on guerrilla warfare in the world. This book, along with certain articles he wrote, in particular his "Guerra de Guerrillas: Un Metodo" ("Guerrilla Warfare: A Method," published in Gerassi 1968a:266–79), provide a complete theory of revolutionary guerrilla warfare, largely based on the Cuban experience. This theory has infl uenced revolutionary movements throughout Latin America and the rest of the world and has inspired many radical groups to start a revolutionary guerrilla *foco* (focal point or center of guerrilla operations) like the one established by Fidel Castro, Che, and their comrades in the Sierra Maestra of Cuba.

D uring his days as a guerrilla leader in the Sierra Maestra, Che made it a habit to write down his daily observations in a personal campaign diary. At the end of a long day's march or after an engagement with the enemy, he always sat down somewhere apart from the others to write about the events of the day. On the basis of these notes he was later able to formulate his theories about guerrilla warfare and to write an excellent historical account of the Cuban revolutionary war, *Pasajes de la Guerra Revolucionaria* (*Episodes of the Revolutionary War,* 1996).

I t was Che's belief that the Cuban Revolution clearly demonstrated that the people of Latin America can liberate themselves from dictatorial rule if they resort to guerrilla warfare. In *La Guerra de Guerrillas* (*Guerrilla Warfare*), Che wrote that the Cuban Revolution had made three fundamental contributions to revolutionary thought in Latin America. First, the Cuban experience proved that popular, irregular forces could win a war against a professional army. Second, it proved that it is not necessary to wait until all the conditions for revolution are present. According to Che, the insurrectional guerrilla foco can itself create the necessary conditions.

T hird, Che believed Cuba demonstrated that, in Latin America, which has a large rural population, a successful revolutionary struggle must initially concentrate on the rural areas and not the cities if it is to succeed. Che claimed that the fi rst two of these contributions refuted the arguments of those who claimed to be revolutionaries but refused to take any revolutionary action because of the pretext that they could not defeat a professional army or because the necessary "objective conditions" for revolution did not exist in Latin America.

H e believed a nucleus of 30 to 50 men could establish and consolidate a revolutionary guerrilla foco in any country of Latin America, providing they were determined, had the cooperation of the people, and had perfect knowledge of the terrain where they would be operating. Che also stressed that the people must believe it is impossible for them to obtain social and economic reforms through peaceful means before they will be inclined to support an insurrectionary guerrilla foco. Moreover, he argued that where a government has risen to power by some form of popular consent, including fraudulent elections, and maintains at least the appearance of constitutional legality, it is impossible to establish and consolidate a guerrilla foco because many of the people will believe that there is some possibility of improving their social and economic conditions through legal means.

C he disagreed with those who argued that the revolutionary struggle in Latin America depended primarily on the political mobilization of the discontented urban masses in the cities. He felt that it was far more diffi cult to carry out a successful insurrection in the cities, where the armed forces and police can be effectively concentrated and utilized, than in the rural areas, where regular troops are at the mercy of a highly mobile guerrilla force supported by the rural population. The support of the rural population, according to Che, is the sine qua non of guerrilla warfare. In fact, he defi ned guerrilla war as a war of the people, led by a fi ghting vanguard (the nuclear guerrilla force) against the forces of the ruling oligarchies (elites) and their foreign backers (the U.S. government and the transnational corporations with investments in the Third World). Thus, in Che's view, the guerrilla force does not seize power by itself; rather, it serves as a catalyst that inspires the people themselves to take up arms and overthrow the established regime.

In *La Guerra de Guerrillas,* Che wrote that without the support of the people a guerrilla force is nothing more than a roving gang of bandits. He noted that both have the same characteristics: homogeneous membership, respect for their leaders, courage, knowledge of the terrain, and appreciation of the correct tactics to employ against numerically superior forces. However, they differ in one fundamental respect: one has the support of the people and the other does not. Consequently, bandits are inevitably hunted down and eliminated, whereas guerrilla forces, which count on the support of the people, can defeat a professional army and bring about the downfall of the most oppressive regime.

A guerrilla force, according to Che, wins the support of the masses in rural areas largely by championing their grievances. This means that the guerrillas must present themselves as crusaders intent on righting the injustices of the prevailing social order. Che believed that the major grievances shared by the rural masses throughout Latin America arose from the concentration of land ownership in the hands of a small, wealthy, landed elite. Thus, the great majority of the peasantry do not own the land on which they live and work. Consequently, he saw land reform as the key issue to be used by guerrilla forces in their effort to win the support of the rural masses. In other words, Che argued that the guerrilla fi ghter must be an agrarian revolutionary who uses the peasantry's hunger for land as the basis for mobilizing its support.

He also believed that any revolutionary guerrilla force must be the conscience of the people, and that the moral behavior of the guerrillas must be such that the people regard them as true priests of the social reforms that they advocate. According to Che, guerrilla fi ghters must always exercise rigid self-control and never permit themselves a single excess or weakness. This means guerrillas must be ascetics whose moral behavior earns them the respect and admiration of the local population. In addition, Che wrote it is the duty of guerrillas to give technical, economic, and social assistance to the peasantry. In this way, they develop a close relationship with the peasantry, which allows them to win their trust and confi dence. Once this relationship has been achieved, it then becomes the task of the guerrillas to indoctrinate the peasantry about the fundamental importance of the armed struggle as the only way they can liberate themselves from their present state of exploitation and oppression. Che believed that the successful execution of this task brings into existence a true people's war and the inevitable destruction of the existing regime.

One of Che's most original contributions to the literature on guerrilla warfare is his discussion of the qualities of the guerrilla fi ghter. According to him, the ideal guerrilla soldier is an inhabitant of the zone where the nuclear guerrilla foco is established. This is because the two most important prerequisites of successful guerrilla warfare are a thorough knowledge of the terrain and the cooperation of the local population. The guerrilla who inhabits the region where he or she operates knows the terrain and has friends in the area to turn to for help. It follows, therefore, that in Latin America the local campesino (peasant) makes the best guerrilla soldier, although Che emphasized that a guerrilla force should not be composed exclusively of campesinos .

Che seems to have been describing himself without knowing it when he listed the personal qualities that the ideal guerrilla soldier should have. He stressed audacity and a readiness to take an optimistic attitude at times when an analysis of existing conditions does not warrant it. He also believed that the guerrilla fi ghter must be ready to risk his or her life almost daily and to voluntarily give it up if the circumstances require it. This of course demands a high degree of devotion to the cause for which the guerrillas are fi ghting, and according to Che, such devotion can be sustained only if the guerrilla movement is based on ideals that are meaningful to each guerrilla fi ghter. He concluded that among nearly all campesinos such an ideal is the right to have a piece of land of their own, while the ideal of adequate wages and better social conditions plays a comparable role among guerrillas from the urban working classes and more abstract ideals, such as political freedom and social equality, motivate students and intellectuals.

I n addition to the moral and psychological qualities that make a good guerrilla fi ghter, Che stressed that guerrillas must also have certain important physical qualities and be able to adapt to the most diffi cult environmental conditions. As Che knew well from his own experience, the conditions of guerrilla life require enduring severe privations, including the lack of food, water, proper clothing, shelter, and medical attention. Moreover, guerrillas must be able to adapt to a life of almost constant movement, in which they are required to march long distances and traverse areas no ordinary man or woman would ever venture.

Che wrote that in terms of the general pattern of a guerrilla's day-today life, combat is the most interesting event. Combat, therefore, is both the climax and the greatest joy in that life, only combat provides the means to fulfi ll the purpose for which the guerrilla exists. Che emphasized that guerrillas must perform their role as combatants without any reluctance or weakness, since they must give the enemy no quarter and expect none in return. On the other hand, Che also made the point that wounded and captured enemy soldiers must be treated benevolently by guerrilla soldiers, unless they have committed criminal acts that require they be tried and perhaps executed.

The fi nal objective of a revolutionary guerrilla war according to Che's perspective is the defeat of the enemy's army and the seizure of political power in the name of the people. However, he made it quite clear that guerrilla warfare cannot in itself bring about victory. He emphasized that it is important to remember that guerrilla warfare is only the fi rst phase of a war of national liberation and that, unless it develops into a conventional war, the enemy cannot be completely defeated.

Che wrote that in a revolutionary guerrilla war's earliest stages the primary strategy of the revolutionary guerrilla force is to assure its own survival. This means that it must fl ee from and avoid the enemy forces sent to destroy it. During this phase, it must restrict its offensive activities to lightning attacks on unsuspecting enemy posts or units and in each case retreat to a secure hiding place before the enemy has a chance to react with its superior forces and weapons. If the guerrilla force succeeded in eluding the enemy forces sent to destroy it, Che assumed it would increasingly attract recruits from the rural population and gradually enlarge the scale of its operations, striking more frequently at the enemy troops in the zone surrounding the guerrilla foco. In this way, the guerrillas begin to weaken and demoralize the enemy's forces. By systematically harassing the enemy through surprise attacks, they also disrupt communications and force the enemy onto the defensive.

T he next phase involves extending the territory of guerrilla activity by sending small groups deep into enemy territory to sabotage and terrorize the enemy's key centers of supply and communications. Meanwhile, the original base of guerrilla operations must be continually strengthened and measures must be taken to indoctrinate the inhabitants of the guerrilla zone. Later, when more fi ghters and arms have been obtained and the circumstances appear to warrant an expansion of the confl ict, new guerrilla columns are formed and sent to operate in areas behind the enemy's lines.

The fi nal phase of the struggle begins, according to Che, when the guerrilla columns unite and engage the enemy's forces in a conventional war of fi xed fronts. It is at this moment that the people's army comes into existence and the drive toward the cities begins. The death knell of the old order comes as the urban masses turn on the defending troops and the last strongholds of enemy resistance surrender to the people's army. This clears the way for the revolutionary leaders to seize power and begin the building of a new society. "Above all it must be made clear that this type of struggle is a method: a method for achieving a purpose. That purpose, indispensable and unavoidable for every revolutionary, is the conquest of political power" (Guevara 1963).

C he warned that a people's army does not emerge spontaneously and that victory is obtained only after a long and diffi cult struggle in which the people's forces and their leaders are exposed to repeated attacks by superior forces intent on annihilating them. He also pointed out that the guerrillas must expect to suffer greatly at the hands of the enemy. Che made this point most effectively in the following passage from his article "Guerrilla Warfare: A Method," which prophetically describes the situation his guerrilla force encountered in Bolivia:

T he enemy army will punish them severely. At times they will be split up into groups, and those who fall prisoner will be tortured.

They will be hounded relentlessly like hunted animals in the areas they have chosen for their operation. They will suffer the constant uneasiness of having enemies at their heels, and they will constantly have to suspect all they encounter, since the frightened peasants will in some instances hand them over to the repressive troops in order to rid themselves of the latter by removing the reason for their presence. Their only alternative will be death or victory, at times when death is a thousand times present and victory is a myth about which only a revolutionary can dream. (in Gerassi 1968:276)

However, Che argued that even if only a fragment of the original guerrilla nucleus survives, it can continue to spark the revolutionary spirit of the masses and can organize anew to carry on the struggle.

Che believed that war is subject to a series of scientifi c laws and that those who disregard these laws are destined to be defeated. Since guerrilla warfare is merely one type of war, he claimed that it was governed by the same laws. However, because of its special aspects, Che argued that guerrilla warfare is also governed by a series of accessory laws or principles that must be recognized by a guerrilla force hoping to succeed.

S ince one of the precepts of guerrilla warfare is the enemy's vast superiority in troops as well as in equipment,

Che stressed that the guerrillas must utilize special tactics that allow them to offset the enemy's superiority in troops and equipment. These tactics are based, as already mentioned, on two essential preconditions: (1) the guerrillas must be highly mobile, and (2) they must possess a much greater knowledge of the terrain than the enemy.

Extreme mobility and a detailed knowledge of the terrain of operations make it possible, in Che's opinion, for the guerrillas to outmaneuver and surprise the numerically superior and better-equipped forces sent against them. With these capabilities, they can strike when the enemy is off guard and then quickly disappear before retaliation, thus infl icting heavy casualties on the enemy with very few or no losses of their own. "Strike and run, wait, watch carefully, and then again strike and run" (Guevara 1963). This, in Che's words, is the primary tactic of guerrilla warfare, to be repeated over and over until the enemy is demoralized and forced to take a static and essentially defensive posture.

The basic characteristics of this tactic are the element of surprise and the rapidity of the guerrillas' attacking and withdrawal maneuvers. The speed and surprise inherent in this tactic give the guerrillas a great advantage over the enemy's larger and better-equipped forces. Moreover, Che noted that it is particularly effective when used at night and that, for this reason, one of the basic features of guerrilla warfare is night fi ghting.

S omewhat more static than the hit-and-run technique, but just as effectivc, is the ambush. This tactic is, of course, as old as war itself and has always been used by the weak against the strong. It requires that the enemy be on the move, ideally marching in fi le through a ravine, canyon, or pass, where the forces can be caught in a devastating crossfi re. However, Che made an original contribution to this age-old tactic. In his writings, Che mentions the psychological damage infl icted on the enemy if the guerrillas always concentrate their fi re on the advance elements of the army units they ambush. The enemy's soldiers realize they can expect almost certain death if they are in the advance positions of a column. This tactic, Che claimed, creates panic among the soldiers and may even lead them to mutiny if they are ordered to take the lead positions in a column marching through a suspected guerrilla area.

In addition to the ambush and the rapid hit-and-run type of attack, Che also wrote about what is called the "minuet tactic." Somewhat analogous to the dance of the same name, this tactic involves surrounding an enemy column with several small groups. These groups alternately engage the enemy from different points. As soon as one group retreats, another one initiates an attack from a different direction. As a result, the enemy column is constantly kept off balance and demoralized. In fact, if the guerrillas have enough men and ammunition and there is no possibility of the surrounded enemy column receiving outside aid, the guerrillas can annihilate the entire column.

Che emphasized that a guerrilla force must never allow itself to be encircled, for experience had shown, he said, that the only really effective way of stamping out a guerrilla force is to encircle the guerrillas in a given area, concentrate as many troops in the circle as possible, and progressively close in around the guerrillas until they are liquidated. For this reason, guerrilla warfare is a war without any fi xed front or battle lines. According to Che, the guerrillas must appear and disappear at the enemy's rear, at the fl anks, and in its midst. In the initial stages, guerrillas should rarely attempt to hold a given position, since their concern is to avoid encirclement or a frontal encounter with the enemy's superior forces. Instead, their aim should be to infl ict as many casualties on the enemy's forces as possible without jeopardizing themselves. Confronted with this type of irregular warfare, Che claimed that the enemy's regular army is rendered powerless. Since the army is equipped and trained to fi ght a conventional war or control the street demonstrations of students and workers, it becomes frightened and demoralized when faced with the tactics of the guerrillas.

Since one of the most important aspects of guerrilla warfare is the relationship between the guerrillas and the local population, Che believed that the guerrillas should conduct themselves at all times in the most respectful manner toward civilians. For this reason, he advocated that they always pay for any goods taken, or at least give a certifi cate of debt to be paid at some future date. He also emphasized that the zone of guerrilla operations must never be impoverished by the direct action of the guerrillas and that the local inhabitants must be permitted to sell their products outside the guerrilla zone, except under extreme circumstances. As the guerrilla effort progresses and whole areas of a country come under their control, then, according to Che, the guerrillas must assume responsibility for governing the civilian population and regulating economic activity in the areas under their control.

Although Che believed sabotage was one of the most effective tactics available to a revolutionary guerrilla movement, he was opposed to terrorism per se. He believed that terrorism is a negative weapon that can turn the people against a revolutionary movement. Moreover, in his opinion, the results of terrorist attacks are not worth the cost in lives that they entail. On the other hand, he distinguished sabotage (the destruction of essential industries and public works) from terrorism (the systematic use of violence to coerce the population) and advocated the destruction of nearly everything necessary for normal, modern life, for example, telephone lines, electrical power stations, water mains, sewers, gas pipelines, railroads, and radio and television stations. Yet even in the case of sabotage, Che pointed out that a guerrilla force must consider the social consequences of each act of destruction so as not to cause unnecessary suffering among the urban and rural masses.

For Che, one of the most important characteristics of guerrilla warfare is the difference between the information possessed by the guerrillas and that possessed by the enemy. He saw the situation as one in which the enemy's regular forces must constantly operate in areas where they encounter the sullen silence of the local inhabitants, while the guerrillas can count on a friend in every house who will pass information about the enemy's movements along to the guerrilla headquarters or the guerrilla force operating in the area. Che believed that this is one of the greatest advantages enjoyed by guerrillas and that it should be utilized to the fullest extent.

However, in Che's opinion, a guerrilla force should never confi de too much in the local peasantry, since peasants have a natural tendency to talk to their friends and relatives about everything they see and hear. Moreover, in view of the brutal way the regular troops treat the local population in an area where guerrillas are known to be operating, he warned that it is to be expected that some will give the enemy information about the guerrillas in order to escape torture or mistreatment.

S ince Che conceived of guerrilla warfare as a revolutionary war of the people in which the guerrillas serve as the revolutionary vanguard, he repeatedly emphasized throughout his writings that the support of the masses was crucial to the success of any guerrilla insurgency. Therefore, he was preoccupied with treating in detail how a guerrilla force secures and develops popular support. For this reason, his writings on revolutionary guerrilla war come closer to being a manual on how to organize and successfully execute a popular revolution than a theoretical work on military strategy and tactics.

M ost revolutionary movements in Latin America following the Cuban revolution were based on Che's contention that a small band of from 30 to 50 guerrillas can create the conditions required for a revolutionary victory in any country of Latin America. Most of these movements, including the one directed by Che himself, failed to demonstrate that an insurrectionary guerrilla foco located in a rural area could, by itself, produce a successful popular revolution.

The Cuban revolution was not purely a peasant revolution, mounted by a small guerrilla force that came down out of the mountains to liberate the cities. Che knew this. There is much more to the story of the Cuban Revolution than this. To be sure, the guerrillas were the symbol of the revolution, and they played a crucial role in its development. However, Cuba's urban working and middle classes, who threw their weight behind the guerrillas because of their hatred of the corrupt Batista regime, and the weakness of the Cuban army, which was not enthusiastic about defending the unpopular regime, played decisive roles. Moreover, if Castro had put forward a more radical program of social and economic reforms prior to his seizure of power, the revolutionary movement against Batista would not have been able to acquire the magnitude of popular support that made its victory possible.

I ronically, the international importance and historical signifi cance of the Cuban Revolution may well have made another Cuban-style revolution in Latin America very diffi cult to achieve. It is hard to imagine a similar revolutionary guerrilla movement today either (1) deceiving the upper and middle classes into believing it has moderate political aims, or (2) winning the support of U.S. and international public opinion as romantic freedom fi ghters combating a tyrannical regime. The political elites in Latin America have learned a lot from the Cuban Revolution and subsequent attempts to replicate it. They now know that a revolutionary guerrilla force must be eliminated as soon as it appears, that the army must be effectively trained in counterinsurgency warfare, and that serious efforts must be made to win the support of the peasantry or at least to forestall their giving support to a revolutionary movement.

However, Che's theory of revolutionary guerrilla warfare overemphasized the importance of the rural population as the popular base for a successful revolutionary movement in Latin America. The armies of a number of Latin American countries, using modern counterinsurgency tactics that their offi cers have learned from U.S. advisors and training programs, have shown that they can defeat or at least contain Cubanstyle revolutionary guerrilla movements that rely principally on a rural base of support.

B ut even more important is the obvious fact, recognized by most Latin Americans interested in revolution, that the main breeding grounds for any kind of radical popular movement in Latin America are the cities and towns. The cities are inundated with migrants from the rural areas. Hoping to break away from the poverty and misery of rural Latin America, they generally fi nd waiting for them in the cities unemployment and worse living conditions than they had in the rural areas. The frustration and discontent that derive from this situation provide a fertile soil for radical political groups. Thus, today and in the future, the exploding urban centers offer an important base of potential popular support for radical political movements in Latin America and in other parts of the world with similar social and economic conditions.

N evertheless, it is important to note that in a modifi ed form Che's ideas on guerrilla warfare and the Cuban model of the catalytic guerrilla foco were adopted with some success by armed revolutionary movements in Central America in the 1970s and the 1980s. The success of the Sandinista Front for National Liberation (Frente Sandinista de Liberación Nacional, or FSLN) in overthrowing the Somoza dictatorship in Nicaragua at the end of the 1970s is perhaps the best example of a successful revolutionary movement in Latin America that began with a rural-based guerrilla force similar to that recommended by Che. However, the FSLN, which was backed by Che and the Cubans in the sixties, succeeded in overthrowing the Somoza regime in the 1970s because it combined guerrilla warfare in the countryside with a successful campaign of urban guerrilla warfare and the development of a multiclass, multiparty political alliance—not that different from what occurred in Cuba. This broad-based political alliance helped the FSLN mobilize a nationwide popular insurrection that toppled the Somoza regime (Harris and Vilas 1995).

F or those who believe a rural-based armed insurrection is no longer viable, with the end of the cold war and modern military methods, the surprise appearance on the contemporary scene of the Zapatista revolutionary movement in southern Mexico in the mid-1990s provides clear evidence that guerrilla movements similar to the type advocated by Che Guevara continue to arise in Latin America and other parts of the world where extreme social injustices persist. And the striking resemblance of the Zapatistas' charismatic spokesperson, Subcomandante Marcos, to Che is certainly no accident of history. Not only does Marcos project a revolutionary persona modeled to a large degree on Che's iconic revolutionary image but he mentions him frequently in his speeches and interviews. The Zapatista movement has more modest political goals and has used less aggressive military tactics than Che and his comrades, but this revolutionary movement, which has emerged from the largely rural, indigenous peasant population of the state of Chiapas clearly refl ects the legacy of Che's revolutionary example. Many of his ideas about imperialism, revolution, socialism, and guerrilla warfare have clearly infl uenced the ideology and tactics of this revolutionary movement (Anderson 1997:753). The relative success and international attention given to this movement have also helped to create renewed interest in Che's ideas about revolutionary guerrilla warfare.